How to Identify Grasses
and Grasslike Plants

SWALLOW PRESS

OHIO UNIVERSITY PRESS

ATHENS

How to Identify Grasses & Grasslike Plants

Sedges and Rushes

H. D. Harrington

Illustrated by Ann Steely,
Robin Hause and Janet Klein

Swallow Press / Ohio University Press books are
printed on acid-free paper ∞

Library of Congress Catalog Card Number: 76-17744
ISBN: 0-8040-0746-2

The Identification of Grasses

A grass can be "glumey" in more ways than one,
When its classification remains to be done;
You pull off the parts, and soon feel your age
Chasing them over the microscope stage!

You peer through the lenses at all of the bracts
And hope your decisions agree with the facts;
While your oculist chortles with avid delight
As you strain both your eyes in the dim table light.

You are left on the horns of quite a dilemma
When you count the nerves on the back of the lemma;
Then you really get snoopy and turn each one turtle
To see if the flower is sterile or fertile.

And then the compression, no problem is meaner —
Is it flat like your wallet or round like a wiener?
"How simple," you think, "for a mind that is keen" —
But what do you do when it's half-way between?

You probe and you guess how the florets will shatter,
For you know later on it is certain to matter;
You long for the calmness of labor that's manual
When the question arises — "perennial" or "annual"?

And that terrible texture, the meanest of all,
Is one of the pitfalls in which you can fall;
"Cartilaginous" maybe — or is it "chartaceous"?
Has even the experts exclaiming "Good gracious!"

Then you wail as you wade through the long tribal key,
"Oh, why must this awful thing happen to me?"
"Grasses are easy," our teacher declares,
As he mops off a brow that is crowned with gray hairs!

Contents

Preface

SOME YEARS AGO I wrote *How to Identify Plants**, a guide for
the identification of plants in general. The grasses were intentionally omitted from that publication, mostly because of
lack of space, but with the intention of treating them separately later on. *How to Identify Grasses and Grasslike Plants* at-
tempts to provide this treatment by offering as much practical
help as possible for those attempting to learn the rather specialized technique of identifying these plants. It is based on
the writer's many years of experience in watching several
thousand students acquire this skill.

However, this book in no way promises an "easy way to
identify" the plants included, since this is an impossibility for
grasses, sedges, and rushes. Many of the species look
superficially alike, and, in order to distinguish them accurately, one must be able to check their technical characters.
Visual memory as to their general appearance is very helpful, but it is not always sufficient. You must know not only
"what it is" but also "why it is what it is" before you really
know a grass. In fact, it is often better to know also why it is
not some closely related species! The first two steps necessary are learning to diagnose accurately and learning to
identify efficiently. This will take a reasonable amount of
effort and perseverance.

In this book the procedure followed in dealing with the
necessary technical descriptive terms is to present the commonly used ones in the initial chapters. These common

---

*1957. Chicago: The Swallow Press

terms really should be memorized eventually as it just takes too long to look each one up every time it is needed. Then the more uncommon terms can be readily checked when encountered by using the illustrated glossary that makes up the last chapter. This chapter also serves as a kind of "index" as the terms are alphabetically arranged.

As this book is not intended as a discussion of theoretical concepts, the definitions of many terms have been very deliberately simplified. The real test was exactly how the terms were actually used in the common manuals. The drawings are designed mainly to clarify the definitions; these latter should always have the final word. However, while sketches can help in presenting the general concept, they obviously cannot illustrate the entire range of variation. In general, the drawings in this book attempt to express a typical, or average, appearance. They have been kept simple and are not drawn from actual plant specimens, since we have no way of knowing just what plant you will be trying to identify when you need information on a certain item!

Finally, I would like to add this warning. You will find this book of practical assistance, but the real work must be done by yourself. There is no "royal road" to learning to identify grasses, sedges, and rushes. It is rather consoling, though, to remember that many others have toiled down the path before you and have finally reached the goal.

How to Identify Grasses
and Grasslike Plants

Introduction

1. *Size.* The grass family has been variously estimated to contain between 500 to 600 genera and 7,500 to 10,000 species. This places it among the first four or five families of plants in total number of genera and species. However, in numbers of species representative to all regions and in percentage of individual plants present, it easily ranks first. It would be difficult indeed to find a family that would out-rank it in economic importance to mankind.

2. *Civilization.* It has been pointed out many times in many places that the great civilizations of mankind have almost invariably developed in the midst of extensive grasslands.

3. *Food.* The most important food producers are almost exclusively to be found in the grass family. Rice, wheat, maize, barley, rye, and oats all belong here.

4. *Forage.* The whole grazing industry is likely to be based primarily on grasses. These plants also provide a large part of the food and protection for wildlife.

5. *Turf.* The importance of sod in the economy of mankind is well known. The importance of grasses in the formation of turf is also obvious to everyone.

For these reasons, and probably many others, the correct identification of grass species sometimes becomes very important indeed.

WHY IDENTIFICATION IS NECESSARY

1. *Curiosity.* Some kind of name for a new object usually becomes a crying necessity.

2. *Talk and write about a plant.* It is necessary that we give some kind of name to a plant in order to carry on an intelligent coversation about it. Published records call for designations for the plants mentioned in the discussions.

3. *Look up information.* The great storehouse of human knowledge may contain an enormous amount of information about the plant about which you are concerned. All this information becomes available only when the name of the plant is known.

BRIGHT SIDE AND DARK SIDE

As indicated by the poem on page v, the grasses are popularly considered to be relatively hard to identify. Like every other problem, however, it has its dark and bright sides. Let us get the dark side out of the way first. (Bad news first!)

1. *Dark Side*

(1) Grasses and grasslike plants constitute a large group with many of the genera containing large numbers of species (like *Poa, Panicum, Muhlenbergia, Juncus,* and *Carex.*) These large groups tend to pose certain problems, if only because of the sheer weight of the numbers involved.

(2) New terms and concepts are always freely used. Students who are accustomed to the terminology of identifying ordinary plants sometimes become bewildered when they first tackle the group.

(3) There may be special meanings to old familiar terms, like "spikelet" and "floret." These concepts must be mastered before much progress can be made in identification.

(4) Grasses do intergrade a great deal, perhaps more so than do the average groups of plants. This makes for continual changes in classification, with many genera shifted about among various tribes and often the species transferred from one genus to another. When only one manual is followed, this is not a significant problem.

(5) Underground parts are often necessary. Sometimes these are not available to you for one reason or another. Every grass specimen collected should indicate in some way, first, whether or not rhizomes were present, and secondly, whether the plant was an annual or perennial. This can be done by selecting a specimen to indicate the characters, or by stating the situation on the label— ideally by doing both!

2. *Bright side* (Now for the good news!)

(1) Grasses can be identified about as well in dry as in fresh condition. This is a great advantage when the specimen is likely to be sent in for checking at any season, or the collecting equipment at hand happens to be primitive. Many of us have learned, somewhat to our surprise, that grasses can be identified using unpressed material as well or even better than material pressed in the conventional manner. We have found this is a great help in collecting class material! Also, grasses dry more readily than do ordinary plants, both in the plant press and outside it.

(2) Grasses can be collected and identified during a much longer season than most of the other plant groups. Of course, the ideal time is just when some of the fruits are starting to fall.

(3) Grasses are of great economic importance and their correct identification may become of great significance. This may provide additional incentive.

(4) Because of this, special treatments of the group are often available for local areas. These often give valuable help in identifying the material.

To summarize the matter, grasses and grasslike plants constitute an important part of the flora of an area and someone somewhere must be able to identify them. Most of these workers we have observed throughout many years soon find out by experience that they would just as soon work with these special groups as with plants in general. Our advice is: Don't get discouraged at the outset!

TREATMENT HERE SPECIALIZED

1. The information contained in this treatment on grasses is related to their identification only.

2. The terms presented are defined in the specialized way that they are used in Agrostology (the study of grasses and their grasslike relatives).

TERMS

1. Special attention is given here to those terms that are of particular significance in the families involved.

2. We suggest again that you memorize the common ones as treated in the first few chapters, and look up those less commonly used in this book's glossary.

EQUIPMENT

1. *Manual or key.* Good sources are listed in Chapter VIII.

2. *Lenses.* They include a good hand lens of the type pictured in Figure 0-1. An 8x (magnification) to 12x is a good strength; a higher magnification is not very practical. High magnification usually necessitates using some kind of dissecting microscope. (See Figure 0-2.)

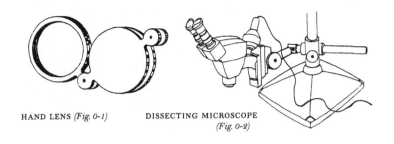

HAND LENS *(Fig. 0-1)*   DISSECTING MICROSCOPE
(Fig. 0-2)

3. Measuring square and rule. It is sometimes desirable to have these graduated to half-millimeters, but it is not always possible to secure them. (Figures 0-3a, 0-3b.)

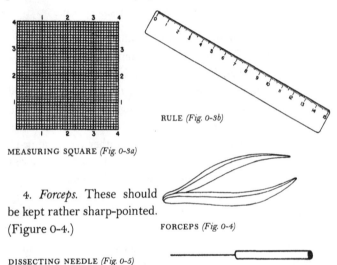

RULE *(Fig. 0-3b)*

MEASURING SQUARE *(Fig. 0-3a)*

4. Forceps. These should be kept rather sharp-pointed. (Figure 0-4.)

FORCEPS *(Fig. 0-4)*

DISSECTING NEEDLE *(Fig. 0-5)*

5. Needles. These come in handy to manipulate small spikelet parts. (Figure 0-5.)

The small bracts of the spikelet have a way of "jumping" around when manipulated, especially when they are dry and static electricity is a problem. Several of our students in past years have intimated that they felt they should receive "physical education" credits for the course in Agrostology! Wetting the dry bracts with water or with a detergent solution may help keep them in place on the microscope stage. Few of us take time to do this; however, double sticky tape has also been used by some.

1. *Species and genus.* There are many definitions of "genera" and "species." The simplest and most practical one for students is about as follows: "Any plant keying down to and fitting the description reasonably well of a certain entity as treated in the manual used."

2. *Common names.* These are names that have come into general use, are usually rather easy to remember, and are often remarkably descriptive of the plant. However, there is little or no order or method about them, at least any in general use, especially for grasses and grasslike plants.

3. *Scientific names.* These are organized according to definite laws and rules, international in application. These names do vary somewhat, due to differences in individual judgment, but it is seldom confusing as to just what plant is really meant. Scientific names are often long and tend to be made up of unusual, unfamiliar syllables. This may make them hard to remember, and may even be rather frightening to some folks. The more work you do with plants, the more you come to respect and rely on these scientific names.

If you are dealing with people not accustomed to hearing the scientific names of plants, it would be folly to use them exclusively. You must speak the people's language. If you do use their common names, never argue about one of them— remember that one common name is as "legal" as another.

All records of vegetation and all published lists should be in botanical terminology. I have read scores of articles about some plant, the exact species of which could not be absolutely ascertained from the text. Use the common name when you wish, but append somewhere the scientific name of the plant, even if it is placed inconspicuously. No matter how careful your observations may be, the value of your work may be partially or completely nullified if the reader cannot discover just what the plant really is that you are talking about! This common name and scientific name problem is discussed at some length in Chapter III of my book, *How to Identify Plants.*

I

Vegetative Morphology of Grasses

ROOTS

1. The roots of grasses are rather small in diameter and are of the fibrous type. (Figure 1-1.)

2. Grasses in general have rather shallow roots although some do extend down for several feet and are remarkably extensive in the soil.

3. The primary root system develops from the radicle. (See Chapter II, "Fruit.") This will sometimes be called simply "primary root." It seldom persists in the mature plant to any extent.

4. Instead the bulk of the roots usually arise as "adventitious" roots from the shoot that is developed from the plumule. (See Chapter II, "Fruit.") These roots constitute what has been

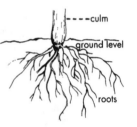

FIBROUS ROOTS *(Fig. 1-1)*

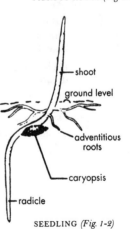

SEEDLING *(Fig. 1-2)*

called the secondary roots or the secondary root system. (Figure 1-2.)

5. The actual roots are little used in the classification of grasses, although the other underground characters (like rhizomes) may be of great value. Roots are generally hidden below ground, and we tend to ignore them.

STEMS

These specialized structures are called "culms" in grasses.

STRICT CULM

(Fig. 1-3)

1. *Grass culms* vary in size from a few centimeters tall to woody bamboos many meters in height.

2. *Their position* in relation to the ground level may be of diagnostic value and seems to be remarkably constant even under variable conditions. Some of the common types are listed next.

(1) *Strict.* A culm rigidly upright. (Figure 1-3.)

(2) *Prostrate.* A culm lying flat on the ground, often rooting at the node but otherwise not particularly differentiated. See also *stolon.* (Figure 1-4.)

PROSTRATE CULM *(Fig. 1-4)*

(3) *Decumbent.* A culm reclining on the ground but turning upward near the end. (Figure 1-5.) Sometimes the books say "culms decumbent at base" when the reclining portion is relatively short.

DECUMBENT CULM *(Fig. 1-5)*

(4) *Ascending.* A culm growing obliquely upward at about a 40°–60° angle from the horizontal, often curved as shown. (Figure 1-6.)

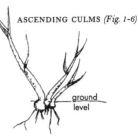

ASCENDING CULMS *(Fig. 1-6)*

ground level

(5) *Caespitose.* Culms growing in tufts or close clusters. The term is rather loosely used and is also written "cespitose." (Figure 1-7.)

CAESPITOSE *(Fig. 1-7)*

(6) *Intravaginal.* This is a term sometimes used for branch culms that push out at the very top of the sheath. The term is little used in identification. (Figure 1-8.)

INTRAVAGINAL *(Fig. 1-8)*

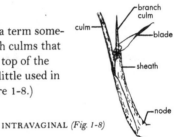

branch culm

culm

blade

sheath

node

(7) *Extravaginal.* This is a type of branching where the branch culm breaks out of the sheath before it reaches the top. (Figure 1-9.)

EXTRAVAGINAL *(Fig. 1-9)*

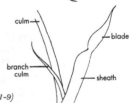

culm

blade

branch culm

sheath

node

(8) *Corm.* This is a short, thickened structure for food storage usually located near or below the ground level. (Figure 1-10.) It may also be called a bulb, and the two terms are often loosely used, especially for grasses.

CORM *(Fig. 1-10)*

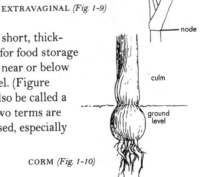

culm

ground level

(9) *Rhizome.* A prostrate, more or less horizontally elongated culm growing partly or completely below the surface, usually rooting at the nodes and becoming upcurved at the apex. It bears modified leaves (scales) on the young growth or scale scars on the older

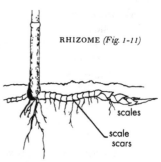

RHIZOME *(Fig. 1-11)*

scales

scale scars

growth. It is often called a "rootstock." The presence or absence of rhizomes is often of great importance in grass identification and should always be checked for when the grass is collected. (Figure 1-11.)

(10) *Stolon.* A specialized, often elongated culm trailing on the ground and rooting at the nodes. A stolon tends to intergrade with a "prostrate" culm. (Figure 1-12.)

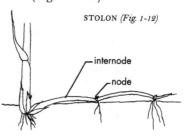

STOLON *(Fig. 1-12)*

internode

node

(11) *False rhizomes.* These structures are so designated here for want of a better name. They are borne on a very loosely caespitose clump where the outer culms run horizontally or ascending for a short distance, even sometimes rooting at the lower nodes. Thus they may remind one of a short rhizome, especially in their young growth. (Figure 1-13.)

(12) *Annual culm.* A culm that dies down to the ground level at the end of the growing season. Most of our grasses are of this type. (The grass itself may be annual or perennial.)

FALSE RHIZOME *(Fig. 1-13)*

(13) *Perennial culm.* This persists and usually becomes woody like a bamboo.

(14) *Annual or Perennial Plants.* This is an important determination to make in identifying many plants of these
groups. In many large genera these two characters actually form main headings in the specific key. The following statements may be of help:

(1) Woody plants are always perennial.

(2) Plants with special organs for food storage such as
tubers, bulbs, corms, rhizomes, etc. are of course
perennial.

(3) Plants with remnants of last year's culms or leaves
attached to the crown along with the new green
shoots are perennials. (Be
careful that your plant isn't
an annual late in the season
where the early culms have
been cut, burned, or grazed
off. In such a case these
early culms may, by con-
trast with the new shoots,
look old and weathered.)
(Figure 1-14.)

PERENNIAL PLANT *(Fig. 1-14)*

(4) Plants that have rather enlarged, thickened structures
at the crown are perennials. The roots of grasses are
not thick enough to store enough food for next
year's growth. Such food is often stored in these
thickened crowns. Some workers claim that they can
determine a perennial by pinching the crown between thumb and fingers. Remember this thickening
is not really bulky. Also
dried mud or embedded
stones can fool you.

(5) Annual grasses stool out
under favorable conditions,
and the culms may become
astonishingly husky.
(Figure 1-15.)

An excellent way to de-
velop this concept is to check
the annual or perennial char-

ANNUAL PLANT *(Fig. 1-15)*

acter of every plant identified as it is listed in the
manual, even though that character may not have

been used in the key. After some experience the
character becomes distinct in almost all cases.

LEAF PARTS *(Fig. 1-16)*

LEAVES

1. *Parts* (Figure 1-16.)

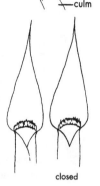

(1) *Sheaths.* These may be *open* or
closed for at least a part of
their length. (Figure 1-17.)

(2) *Auricles.* These ear-like structures
extend from the lower edge of the
blade. They may be present only on
some of the leaves or absent entirely.
(Figure 1-18.)

(3) *Ligules.* These are collar-like structures situated on the leaf at the junction of the blade and the sheath. The
ligule may be a *membrane*, made up
of *hairs*, or part of both (membrane
at base, hairy at apex), and its shape
and length are remarkably constant
for a vegetative character. (Figure 1-19.)

closed

CLOSED *(Fig. 1-17)*

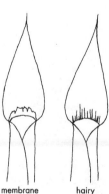

membrane   hairy   LIGULES *(Fig. 1-19)*

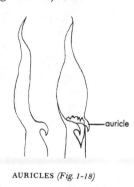

AURICLES *(Fig. 1-18)*

(4) *Collar.* This is a band of cells usually lighter-colored than the surrounding tissue that lies back of the *ligule* and at the base of the blade. It is best seen when the leaf is viewed from the back. (Figure 1-20.)

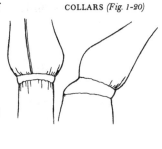

COLLARS *(Fig. 1-20)*

(5) *Blade.* The leaf blades are usually narrowly linear in shape. They are two-ranked on the stem, although this may be more or less obscured by the twisting of the culm in its growth. The shape of the blade in cross-section has some value in classification.

(a) *Flat.* Such a condition may be somewhat obscured when the grass dries up but usually shows up where the blade has been bent. (Figure 1-21.)

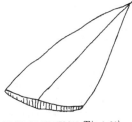

FLAT IN SECTION *(Fig. 1-21)*

(b) *Conduplicate.* Here the blade is folded lengthwise on the midrib. It may be called simply "folded." (Figure 1-22.)

CONDUPLICATE *(Fig. 1-22)*

(c) *Involute.* Here the blade is rolled on the upper surface in from the edges. This term is loosely used in most manuals to include any blade rolled lengthwise in any fashion. Therefore a blade that is *revolute* or *convolute* is apt to be called "*involute*." (Figure 1-23.)

INVOLUTE *(Fig. 1-23)*

(d) *Convolute.* Defined as rolled on the upper or lower surface with one edge enclosed by the other. (Figure 1-24.) The term is loosely used in grasses. See also *involute.*

CONVOLUTE *(Fig. 1-24)*

(e) *Revolute.* Like *involute*, but rolled in on the lower surface. Loosely used. See also *involute.* (Figure 1-25.)

REVOLUTE *(Fig. 1-25)*

As suggested before, the shape of the blade in cross-section is often used in grass identification. A few grasses like corn (*Zea mays*) roll in their leaf blades in times of drought and unroll them when the moisture conditions are more favorable. Fortunately, native grasses are rather constant in this character under all conditions (flat or rolled), and it is a character commonly used in the keys.

2. *Modified Leaves*

(1) *Scale.* This is a leaf reduced to a scale or chaff. In grasses it is used for such structures borne below the foliage leaves, as on the base of the culms or on the younger rhizomes. (Figure 1-26.) See special use of this term in Chapter VI.

(2) *Bracts.* These are modified, more or less reduced leaves. In grasses they are located above the foliage leaves. (See *scale, glume, lemma,* and *palea.*)

(3) *Involucre.* A whorl or circle of bracts. These may be more or less fused to each other and need not be exactly equal or in a perfect whorl. (Figure 1-27.)

(4) *Spines.* Rarely the leaves are modified to form sharp-pointed spines.

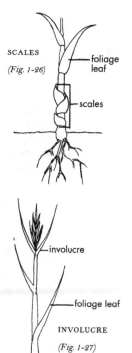

SCALES *(Fig. 1-26)* — foliage leaf — scales

INVOLUCRE *(Fig. 1-27)* — involucre — foliage leaf

(5) *Prophyllum.* The reduced first leaf of a branch culm. It is rarely used in the identification. Since it is two-nerved or two-keeled, it has been compared to the *palea.* (Figure 1-28.)

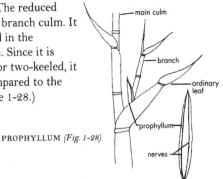

PROPHYLLUM *(Fig. 1-28)*

3. Surfaces

The rather difficult surface terms used in general identification are discussed, illustrated, and keyed out in Chapter IX of the book *How to Identify Plants.* These terms are greatly simplified in the study of grasses and only the few important ones are dealt with here.

(1) *Glabrous.* No hairs of any kind present or any other unusual characteristics.

(2) *Glaucus.* Covered with a whitish, often waxy covering. This may rub off, showing the normal color beneath (usually green), but in grasses the term is used for any whitish surface.

(3) *Pubescent.* With short to medium length hairs. The term is often loosely used to refer to a hairy surface of any kind, especially contrasted to *glabrous.* (Figure 1-29.)

PUBESCENT *(Fig. 1-29)*

A surface with very short hairs is called *puberlent.*

(4) *Pilose.* With long, soft, nearly straight hairs. When the hairs are somewhat wavy, it may be called *villous,* but the two terms are used interchangeably in many books on grasses. (Figure 1-30.)

PILOSE *(Fig. 1-30)*

(5) *Scabrous.* Rough and rasp-like when rubbed gently with the fingertip. This roughness may be caused by short, stiff hairs or short, sharp projections. (Figure 1-31.)

SCABROUS *(Fig. 1-31)*

(6) *Hirsute.* With long, moderately stiff hairs. Very stiff hairs would be *hispid.* (Figure 1-32.)

HIRSUTE *(Fig. 1-32)*

(7) *Ciliate.* Beset with a marginal fringe of hairs, these more conspicuous than any surface hairs that may be present. (Figure 1-33.)

(8) *Antrorse* and *Retrorse.* These hairs (of any type) are more or less appressed to the surface. *Antrorse* hairs point toward the apex, *retrorse* point toward the base of the structure bearing them.

SHEATH CILIATE *(Fig. 1-33)*

II

Spikelet Morphology of Grasses

SPIKELET: A MODIFIED BRANCH

The spikelet is a modified flowering branch with bracts and flowers. It is a definite unit in almost all cases. (Figure 2-1.).

FLOWERING BRANCH *(Fig. 2-1)*

Definition. The grass spikelet can be simply defined as a unit consisting of two empty bracts (glumes) at the base (one or both sometimes lacking or reduced), subtending one or more *florets.* (Figure 2-2.)

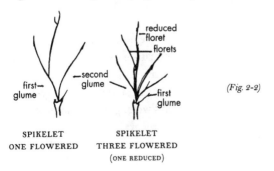

(Fig. 2-2)

SPIKELET
ONE FLOWERED

SPIKELET
THREE FLOWERED
(ONE REDUCED)

Definition. A grass floret is a unit consisting of two bracts (*lemma* and *palea)* which usually enclose a flower (see below). Sometimes the *palea* may be reduced or lacking; the *lemma* may be reduced (still called a floret), but is never lacking entirely. (Figure 2-3.)

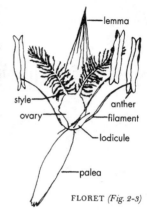

FLORET *(Fig. 2-3)*

FLOWER—TYPES

1. *Perfect.* The perfect grass flower consists of a pistil and three stamens (see *lodicule),* with no definite *perianth* present.

2. *Imperfect.* When stamens only are present, the flower (or floret or spikelet) is called *staminate*; if the pistil only is present, it would be called *pistillate.* When staminate and pistillate flowers are on the same plant (like corn, *Zea mays),* the plant is called *monoecious,* on different plants it is termed *dioecious.* Such imperfect flowers in separate spikelets are not common in grasses.

3. *Sterile.* Any flower lacking a pistil may be called "sterile" in the manuals. Stamens may or may not be present in sterile flowers.

4. *Rudimentary.* A flower part may be greatly reduced.

The flower is seldom examined in identifying grasses except occasionally to decide whether or not a reduced or sterile floret is present. Because the flowers are so little used, one can identify grasses in immature stages before the flower parts are exposed, or in mature fruiting condition when the flowers are past blossoming. As stated previously, this considerably extends the period when grasses can be keyed out, as compared with plants in general.

GLUMES

1. *Number and position.* The glumes are usually two in number. Occasionally one or both may be lacking. There are never more than two; if a third glume-like bract is present, it will be found to be a lemma of a modified floret. The glumes are at the base of the spikelet, next to the pedicel (when one is present).

2. *First and second.* The bracts of a spikelet may be rather crowded, but on close examination they will be found to be two-ranked and alternately arranged; the first glume inserted lower and immediately below the first floret. The first glume is usually somewhat smaller than the second glume. (Figure 2-4.)

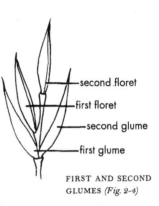

second floret

first floret

second glume

first glume

FIRST AND SECOND
GLUMES *(Fig. 2-4)*

3. *Glume obsolete.* One or both of the glumes may be lacking; if only one is gone, it is always the first lacking.

LEMMA

1. *Most modified.* Of all the bracts, it is the most apt to be modified. For example, the lemmas may be reduced in size, may be unusual in texture (like *hyaline* or *indurated*), or may bear one or more *awns.* When it is not differentiated in any way, the glumes may be.

2. *Last to disappear.* It is the last bract to disappear in the evolutionary modification of the spikelet. (The glumes and the palea go first.)

3. *Arrangement.* They are two-ranked and are situated to the outside of the spikelet (when two or more florets are pres-

ent). The lemma of the first floret is situated directly above the first glume (or where it would be if it were present.) (Figure 2-4.)

4. *Callus.* The base of the lemma is called a *callus,* but the term is seldom used unless this base is modified in some way such as figured. (Figure 2-5.)

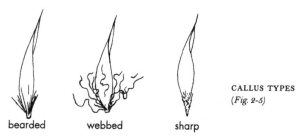

bearded   webbed   sharp

CALLUS TYPES
(*Fig. 2-5*)

PALEA

1. *Position.* This is the inner bract and is usually enclosed by the edge of the lemma (unless the two are spread in anthesis). It lies next to the *rachilla* when one is present.

2. *Nerves.* It is always two-nerved or two-keeled and has been compared with the prophyllum.

3. *Size.* Usually it is nearly as long as its lemma but may be much reduced in size or even lacking entirely.

4. *Value.* The palea is seldom mentioned, but when it is unusual in some way, it has its value in the identification of grasses. (Figure 2-6.)

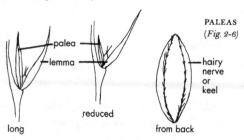

PALEAS
(*Fig. 2-6*)

palea — lemma — reduced

long   from back

hairy nerve or keel

LODICULE

1. *Definition.* These are small bumps or projections.

2. *Number.* They are two in number and are located at the base of the floret, one on each side near the edges of the lemma. (Figure 2-7.)

3. *Function.* By swelling up, the lodicules pry the lemma and palea apart and allow the anthers and styles to protrude when the flower is in *anthesis.*

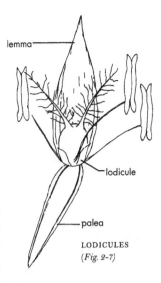

LODICULES
(*Fig. 2-7*)

4. *Homology.* They are thought to be homologous with the *perianth.* They are rarely used in identification.

PISTIL

1. *Number of parts.* The ovary is one-celled with one ovule (at least only one maturing), typically has two styles, each with a feathery stigma as in most wind-pollinated plants. (Figure 2-8.)

2. *Carpels.* According to the general rule of counting the number of styles, stigma lobes, lodicules, and placentae (the highest count giving the number present), there would appear to be two carpels. (Some grass students get three on the basis of other evidence.)

PISTIL
(*Fig. 2-8*)

STAMENS

1. *Number.* These usually number three to a flower, the filaments are slender and the anthers large (as in most wind-pollinated flowers), appearing to be versatile. (Figure 2-9.)

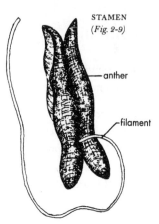

STAMEN
(Fig. 2-9)

— anther

— filament

2. *Value.* The stamens are seldom used in identification unless one wishes to determine if the floret is perfect or staminate. In fact, stamens are usually not present on grass specimens being identified.

FRUIT

1. *Caryopsis.* This is a dry, *indehiscent*, one-seeded fruit in which the ovary wall (pericarp) is united to the seed at all points. Other types of fruit are only rarely present in some unusual grasses.

2. *Special use of the term.* A "fruit" is defined in botany as a matured and developed ovary, sometimes with closely adjacent parts. In grasses, it is the caryopsis and anything that is so closely associated that it happens to fall with it. This structure may be the floret, the spikelet, a group of closely packed spikelets, or even a fused group of *involucre* bracts containing one or more spikelets. (Figures 2-10, 2-11, 2-12.)

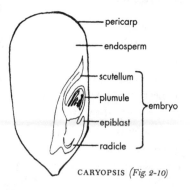

— pericarp

— endosperm

— scutellum ⎤

— plumule ⎥ embryo

— epiblast ⎥

— radicle ⎦

CARYOPSIS *(Fig. 2-10)*

3. *Value of identification.*
The fruits are often very
valuable, especially in indicat-
ing *disarticulation* (see Chapter III)—so much so that
most collectors would rather
collect and identify a grass in
fruit than in flower. The ana-
lysts in seed laboratories must learn to
identify many grasses by their fruits
alone, as they appear in the commer-
cial "seed" with which they work.

FRUIT
(*Fig. 2-11*)

palea

caryopsis

lemma

SEED

SANDBUR (CENCHRUS)
(*Fig. 2-12*)

1. *Special use of the term.* What the farmer and rancher
term "grass seeds" usually turn out to be really "fruits."

2. *Embryo.* It is on the side next to the lemma. Its various
modifications have been much used in the modern
classification of grasses. (See Figure 2-10.)

3. *Scutellum.* Acts as an absorbing organ to transfer food
materials from the endosperm to the developing *radicle* and
plumule. (See Figure 2-10.)

4. *Epiblast.* This is a knob or projection on the side of the
embryo opposite to the *scutellum.* (See Figure 2-10.) It is seldom noticeable and seems to be rarely used in identification.

RACHILLA

1. *Definition.* It is the central axis (little rachis) of the
spikelet. It may be rather long when it bears several florets,
or may be very short, or practically obsolete when only one
floret is present. It may then form a part of the *callus.*

2. *Extension.* The rachilla may extend above the last (or only) floret. In such cases it is often thread-like and can easily be overlooked, especially if the callus or lemma bears stiff hairs. (Figure 2-13.)

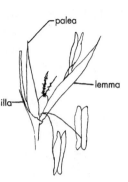

RACHILLA EXTENSION
(Fig. 2-13)

III

Spikelet Modifications of Grasses

To the embryonic student of grasses, this may well be the most helpful chapter in the book. It has been estimated that there are about five hundred genera of grasses in the world, almost all differing from each other in various combinations of spikelet characters. The more important of these various modifications are discussed here with a few suggestions as to how to solve some of the perplexing problems of correct diagnosis. Do not get discouraged if it takes a reasonable amount of time and effort to understand the various modifications of the grass spikelet. We hope this chapter helps you in this!

ENUMERATION OF FLORETS

1. *Variation.* They vary from one spikelet to over fifty in number.

2. *Sterile or reduced.* These structures are counted as florets in determining the total number to a spikelet unless specifically excepted (as "perfect florets one, with sterile floret below," etc.).

MENSURATION

1. *Importance.* The size of the bracts of the spikelet (usually only the length) is very important. Beginning students of grasses are sometimes surprised to learn that a difference of a fraction of a millimeter can affect the identification. A ruler graded to half millimeters comes in handy.

2. *Measuring square.* These squares are very handy in making close measurements. The bracts of the spikelet can be dissected out on the square. This can be done under the very lenses of a dissecting binocular microscope, or the square can be placed later under the magnification for accurate measurement. These measuring squares can be secured at many biological supply houses. (Figure 3-1.)

MEASURING SQUARE
(Fig. 3-1)

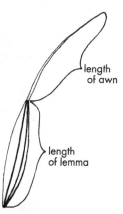

3. *Awn.* The awn, when present, is not counted in on the total length of the bract unless it is very short. This awn length is usually given separately. (Figure 3-2.)

length of awn

4. *Large or small.* In measuring a part in a spikelet, select a rather large one. This seems to be an unwritten law. Do not pick an average or, on the other hand, an abnormally large one.

length of lemma

AWN LENGTH
MEASURED SEPARATELY
(Fig. 3-2)

NERVATION

The number of *nerves* of the bracts is generally very important, and a good lens or a dissecting scope becomes an absolute necessity.

1. *Odd number.* The nerves are practically all odd-numbered on all the bracts except on the palea (where there are almost always two). One main nerve is located at or near the middle of the bract. (Figure 3-3.)

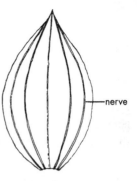

nerve

BACK OF FIVE
NERVED BRACT
(Fig. 3-3)

2. *On a V-shaped bract.* Count the number of nerves on the side facing you, double the number (for those on the other side), then add one for the central nerve and you have the total without the trouble of flattening out the V-shaped bract. (Figure 3-4.)

3. *Nerves on edge.* No nerves are present on the very edge of the bract, although they may appear to be so due to the inrolled edges. (Figure 3-5.)

FIVE NERVED
BRACT
(Fig. 3-4)

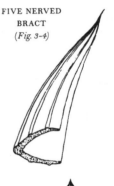

4. *Primary and secondary nerves.* Some nerves are often relatively prominent (primary), and others are weaker (secondary or intermediate). If any at all are prominent, it will ordinarily be the midnerve. (Figure 3-6.)

midnerve

sidenerve
(appears
on edge)

THREE NERVED BRACT WITH
INROLLED EDGES *(Fig. 3-5)*

THREE PRIMARY NERVES
FOUR SECONDARY
NERVES *(Fig. 3-6)*

5. *Light source.* Most workers allow the illumination to come in from the direction of the base of the bract. This seems to make the nerves and surface hairs stand out more clearly, but you can experiment a bit for yourself in this respect.

6. *Parallel or converging nerves.* The converging nerves come together at the apex (or would if they continued on to the pointed apex). Such nerves are associated with the more or less pointed tip. Parallel nerves, on the other hand, are associated with a bract broadly rounded at the apex. (Figure 3-7.)

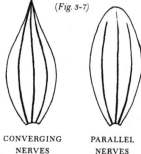

(Fig. 3-7)

CONVERGING NERVES PARALLEL NERVES

COMPRESSION

The spikelets are described as being compressed in two ways, but in many cases appear to be essentially *terete*, not compressed at all. In such cases they may fall in either *lateral* or *dorsal*. This type of compression is used in helping delimit the large groups.

1. *Lateral*

(1) The spikelet is more or less flattened from the sides as shown. (Figure 3-8.)

(2) Usually associated with the lack of sterile or reduced florets in the spikelet, or, if these are present, they are commonly situated above the perfect ones.

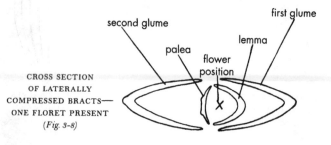

CROSS SECTION OF LATERALLY COMPRESSED BRACTS— ONE FLORET PRESENT *(Fig. 3-8)*

second glume · first glume · lemma · palea · flower position · X

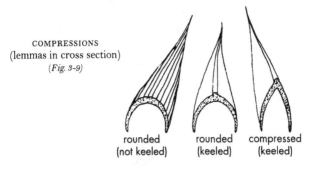

COMPRESSIONS
(lemmas in cross section)
(*Fig. 3-9*)

rounded
(not keeled)

rounded
(keeled)

compressed
(keeled)

(3) In its extreme form, the bracts of a laterally compressed spikelet are compressed keeled. Some common types of compression are shown for bracts (lemma here). (Figure 3-9.)

2. Dorsal

(1) Here the spikelet is more or less compressed from the back of the bracts.

(2) Such spikelets often appear terete, but the perfect floret is usually more clearly dorsally flattened. The diagram is of course exaggerated. (Figure 3-10.)

(3) This dorsal compression is typically associated with the presence

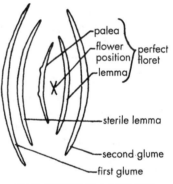

palea
flower position } perfect floret
lemma

sterile lemma

second glume

first glume

CROSS SECTION OF A DORSALLY
COMPRESSED SPIKELET
(*Fig. 3-10*)

of a sterile floret inserted below the perfect one. (This is usually reduced to a lemma that resembles a third glume, which, of course, is not actually present in grasses.) (See Figure 3-10.)

ARTICULATION

1. *Definition.* The articulation is the joint that marks the place where the falling "fruit" pulls away (disarticulates)

from the inflorescence. The two terms "articulating" and "disarticulating" are often used interchangeably. Some common methods of disarticulation are given below.

2. *Above the glumes.*

(1) *This may be directly above the glumes,* the rest of the spikelet (floret or florets) falling together. In the drawing, the spikelet has only one floret, but two or more can be present. (Figure 3-11.)

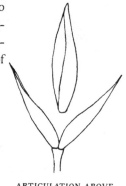

ARTICULATION ABOVE
THE GLUMES
(Fig. 3-11)

(2) *In the rachilla.* The rachilla may break up, letting the florets fall separately. (Figure 3-12.)

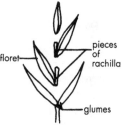

floret

pieces of rachilla

glumes

ARTICULATION
IN THE RACHILLA
(Fig. 3-12)

(3) *Caryopsis with lemma.* Here the caryopsis falls, carrying with it the lemma, leaving the palea still attached to the rachilla, as in Lovegrass (*Eragrostis*). (Figure 3-13.)

(4) *Caryopsis with floret.* Here the lemma and palea both fall with the caryopsis. The spikelet may have one or more florets. (See Figure 3-11.)

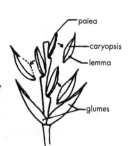

palea

caryopsis

lemma

glumes

CARYOPSIS FALLS
WITH LEMMA
(Fig. 3-13)

(5) *Caryopsis only.* This is where the caryopsis shatters out of its enclosing lemma and palea. An example is in cultivated wheat (*Triticum aestivum*); the character is not at all common in native grasses.

(6) *Seed only*. There the true botanical seed falls from the enclosing *pericarp*, as in dropseed (*Sporobolus*). Of course, this unit is not the usual situation found in most grasses.

ARTICULATION BELOW THE
GLUMES (*Fig. 3-14*)

3. Just below the glumes. The articulation is just below the glumes and the whole spikelet falls as a unit. One or more than one floret may be present to a spikelet in such cases. (Usually one caryopsis is present.) (Figure 3-14.)

4. Group of spikelets. Sometimes two or more spikelets may be closely packed to form a unit that falls together. These may even be united by surrounding structures. (Figure 3-15.)

5. In rachis. The rachis or main axis of the inflorescence (a spike or spike-like one) shatters, and the spikelet (or spikelets, if two or more are present at a node) falls with the joint of the axis. (Figure 3-16.)

HILARIA–GROUP
OF SPIKELETS

(*Fig. 3-15*)

BUCHLOE–GROUP OF
PISTILLATE SPIKELETS

6. How to tell articulation.

(1) The best way is to arrange to collect the plant when the fruits are just beginning to shed. Then all the evidence you need will be at hand, both normal and shattering spikelets. Of course, this is not always possible.

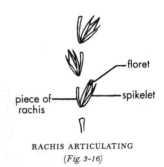

floret

piece of
rachis

spikelet

RACHIS ARTICULATING
(*Fig. 3-16*)

(2) In cases where the fruit is not mature, the articulation can often be observed as a slightly swollen knob or joint marking the place where the parts will later pull apart. This is more readily observable when the articulation is below the glumes. (Figure 3-17.)

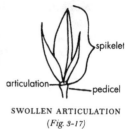

SWOLLEN ARTICULATION
(Fig. 3-17)

(3) One can sometimes probe and manipulate the parts of the spikelets with the fingers or a pair of forceps. Often you can get them to break apart in the manner they will follow naturally, later on. Remember, the parts are rather slender and fragile and your pressure may snap off non-disarticulating structures. However, used with care and caution, this manipulation does help.

DISTRIBUTION

These structures on the bracts seem to be connected (or may have been, in their evolutionary history) with the distribution of the enclosed caryopsis.

1. *Awns.* These are narrow, stiff, bristle-like structures with parallel sides.

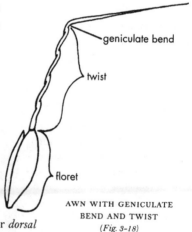

AWN WITH GENICULATE
BEND AND TWIST
(Fig. 3-18)

(1) Usually there is one to a bract. They may be straight, curved, geniculated, or twisted. (Figure 3-18.)

(2) The insertion may be *terminal*, from a *bifid apex*, or *dorsal* or *basal*. (Figure 3-19.)

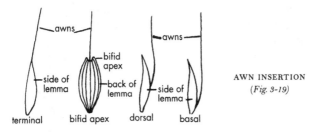

terminal   bifid apex   dorsal   basal

AWN INSERTION
(Fig. 3-19)

(3) Awns are commonest on the lemmas.

2. *Awns pointed.* A common descriptive term that sometimes bothers beginners. They wonder, how long does the point have to be, before it becomes an awn? Usually a structure less than 1 mm. long will be called an "awn point" and over that, an awn. This depends somewhat on the size of the bract. (Figure 3-20.)

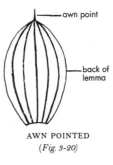

AWN POINTED
(Fig. 3-20)

3. *Length.* The length of the awn is usually not considered to be part of the length of the bract, but is listed separately in most manuals.

PROTECTION

Under this heading are considered the various structures and thickenings that are here arbitrarily considered to protect the caryopsis from possible harm (hail, insects, etc.). This is a little far-fetched, but they are commonly present and are useful in identification.

1. *Upper leaf sheath.* The inflorescence, at least in part, may remain in the sheath. (Figure 3-21.)

2. *Hollow rachis.* Sometimes the

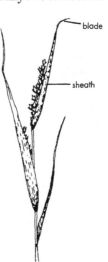

INFLORESCENCE
REMAINS IN SHEATH
(Fig. 3-21)

rachis or axis of the spike is rather hollow on the sides and partly encloses the spikelet. (Figure 3-22.)

STERILE BRANCHES
NEAR SPIKELET
(Fig. 3-23)

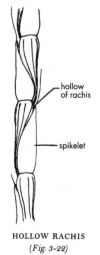

hollow
of rachis

spikelet

HOLLOW RACHIS
(Fig. 3-22)

3. *Sterile branches.* Sometimes the sterile branches of the inflorescence form a kind of enclosing structure. (Figure 3-23.)

SANDBUR *(Fig. 3-24)*

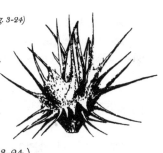

4. *Sterile branches fused.* This is a specialized form of sterile branch. The classic example is the sandbur (*Cenchrus* sp.), which is made of *spinescent,* fused branches enclosing the spikelets. (Figure 3-24.)

5. *Specialized bracts.* In a few cases, a modified, more or less hard-coated bract encloses one or more spikelets. The example is Job's tears (*Coix lacryma-jobi*). (Figure 3-25.)

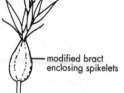

modified bract
enclosing spikelets

COIX LACRYMA-JOBI *(Fig. 3-25)*

6. *Hardened bracts of spikelet.* More commonly, one or more of the bracts of

the spikelet has a hard or thickened coat. These can be on the glumes, the lemma, or the palea. Commonly if the glumes are modified, the lemma and palea are not and vice versa.

7. *Textures.* These are very difficult concepts to master, as definitions are rather inadequate and drawings seem impossible. The best way to learn these textures is to observe numerous representatives. It is suggested you learn the definitions first, then check the recorded texture on every grass identified (this may be given in the generic or the specific description), even though you may not have had to make that decision in keying it out. If the type of texture is not mentioned, it is probably *membranous.* The texture types are usable concepts and begin to make sense after awhile. Do not get discouraged at first.

(1) *Membranous* (or *membranaceous*). This is the ordinary, run-of-the-mill, rather thin texture, the most common of all. The bract is usually green in color and the veins often noticeable. However, it is not real thin and translucent as the name might suggest.

(2) *Hyaline.* Thin, dry, whitish in color, and transparent or translucent.

(3) *Scarious.* Thin, dry, not green but whitish in color. Usually not so translucent as hyaline, but the two terms are used interchangeably by some authors.

(4) *Indurate.* This is the hardest, thickest texture (thick for rather thin spikelet parts). It is usually not green in color and is apt to have a smooth shiny surface.

(5) *Cartilaginous.* Tough, rather thick and elastic like a piece of cartilage.

(6) *Coriaceous.* Thick and tough like a piece of leather. Close to *cartilaginous.*

(7) *Chartaceous.* Of the texture of stiff writing paper (parchment). Someone once suggested that if you place a chartaceous bract under the lens and bear down on the back surface with a sharp-pointed needle, the point is apt to break through without bending the bract. This would not be the case with a *cartilaginous* or *coriaceous* bract, which is tough and more or less elastic.

(Numbers 5, 6, and 7 are difficult terms and are often used loosely in grass manuals.)

REDUCTION

This means the presence of rudimentary or sterile florets somewhere in the spikelet. They are rather common in grasses and it may be difficult at first to master the concepts involved. However, this must be done before a grass spikelet can be accurately diagnosed, a necessary preliminary step to identifying the plant.

1. *Perfect florets.* This is the common situation where stamens and pistil are present on the same flower. If the floret is not modified in any way in size or form, it is fairly safe to assume it was originally perfect. (It may have been collected in fruit with the stamens gone.) Also, if the spikelet contains only one floret, it probably was perfect since *dioecious* and *monoecious* native grasses are rather uncommon.

2. *Modified florets.* These can be suspicioned when unusual bracts (or whole florets) are present. They usually differ in some significant way from the normal perfect ones. Some of these unusual *florets* are given next.

(1) *Staminate.* Contains stamens only while in flower. Such florets may be called "sterile." They usually have undifferentiated lemma and palea, and are often empty when examined, the stamens having been shed.

(2) *Pistillate.* Contains pistils only and may be called "fertile." The bracts are often differentiated in some way and become plump from the developing caryopsis. A pistillate floret is hard to tell from a perfect floret with the stamens shed.

(3) *Lemma and palea only.* No flower parts present in the floret.

(4) *Palea missing.* This is normal in a few grasses.

(5) *Lemma reduced.* It can be greatly reduced in size, shape,

and texture from the normal. It still counts as a floret in the total number to the spikelet. If you find a structure in the spikelet, small or not, that is not a hair or a rachilla (which is more cylindrical), then you may suspect a "reduced" floret, with nothing left but the modified lemma.

3. *Position of modified floret.* These variously modified florets are in two main positions in relation to the perfect ones in the spikelet.

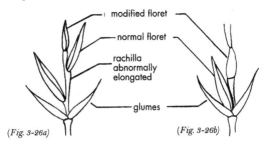

modified floret

normal floret

rachilla abnormally elongated

glumes

(Fig. 3-26a)   *(Fig. 3-26b)*

MODIFIED FLORET ABOVE PERFECT

(1) *Above.* This is fairly common in spikelets with several florets (but possible when two are present; see Figure 3-26b). The end of the rachilla may bear a small, sterile, otherwise normal-looking floret (a) or a highly modified one as shown in b.

(2) *Below.* These reduced florets may resemble a third glume in many cases. They are commonly staminate, or reduced to a sterile lemma. (Figure 3-27.)

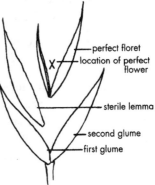

perfect floret

location of perfect flower

sterile lemma

second glume

first glume

REDUCED OR MODIFIED FLORET BELOW PERFECT (DISSECTED)
(Fig. 3-27)

37

IV

Inflorescences of Grasses

The *inflorescence* of grasses is figured on the basis of the spikelets as the units and not the actual flowers as in most other plants.

POSITION

1. *Terminal.* The inflorescence is on the end of the main culms in the majority of cases.

2. *Lateral.* Occasionally the main culm branches above the base and the lateral branches bear inflorescences.

3. *Cleistogamous.* Sometimes the spikelets are completely hidden in the sheaths and never open for pollination. This may happen oftener than suspected because such inflorescences can easily be missed.

TYPES

1. *Spike.* Here one or more spikelets are inserted *sessile* on the central axis (rachis). The spikelets are in two general

rows but these may be twisted around on one side. Most spikes are single on the culm. (Figure 4-1.)

SPIKES *(Fig. 4-1)*

2. *Panicle.* This is the commonest type of inflorescence in grasses. It has a central axis (*main axis* or *rachis*) with primary and secondary branches ending in the pedicels that bear the spikelets. Probably only one true primary branch is present at one node of the central axis. Some grasses like Kentucky Bluegrass (*Poa pratensis*) have these primary branches rebranch from the very base. In such a case, there appears to be more than one at a node. Some types of panicles are as follows.

two ranked   one sided

(1) *Open.* Here the primary and secondary branches are widely spreading to varying degrees. (Figure 4-2.)

(2) *Contracted.* The primary and secondary branches are sometimes rather short and appressed, making a narrow panicle. This is a very usable character and, strangely enough, works best on dried inflorescences. (Figure 4-3.)

A few grasses like Junegrass (*Koeleria cristata*) have their branches contracted when young, spreading in anthesis, then contracted again after pollination. This sometimes bothers workers in the field where a "familiar" grass may look unusual in flower. The

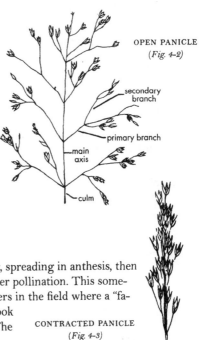

OPEN PANICLE
(Fig. 4-2)

secondary branch

primary branch

main axis

culm

CONTRACTED PANICLE
(Fig. 4-3)

movement in spreading and contracting the branches is caused by small, rather swollen motor organs called *pulvini* located at the base of the branches. Fortunately, this opening and closing is not common. (Figure 4–4.)

3. *Spikelike.* Here the branches are very short and the spikelets close-packed as shown. An example is a timothy "head" (*Phleum pratense*) which can be shown by dissection to actually be a panicle. (Figure 4–5.)

4. *Raceme.* Such an inflorescence, where the first branches off the rachis bear the spikelets, is not common in grasses except in a very modified form. Sometimes several spikelike racemes arise from along the central axis and are often called "racemes of the panicle." (Figure 4–6.)

--- main axis

---primary branch

pulvinus

PULVINUS
(*Fig. 4-4*)

SPIKELIKE PANICLE
(*Fig. 4-5*)

BISEXUAL OR UNISEXUAL

The whole inflorescence may be made up of spikelets with bisexual florets, unisexual and bisexual florets mixed, or unisexual florets only. In the latter case the inflorescence may be "staminate" or "pistillate" as in corn (*Zea mays*) "tassel" and "ear."

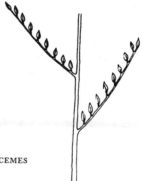

PANICLE OF RACEMES
(*Fig. 4-6*)

V

Collecting and Pressing

The following suggestions are more or less specific for the grasses and their relatives. For more general directions than are given here, see Chapter XIII of *How to Identify Plants*.

VALUE OF COLLECTING AND PRESSING

1. *To learn plants.*

(1) Collecting and pressing is the very best way to learn the plants of an area quickly; otherwise, the recently collected plants have a way of crowding out the earlier ones from your mind. You get to see the plants several times in the pressing and mounting process, and, while the plant may look somewhat different growing in the field, a dried specimen calls to mind very nicely its previous appearance. This is particularly the case if you have pressed and mounted the plant yourself and appreciate exactly what happens in the process.

(2) Collecting specimens allows you to "collect now and identify later." The plants of an area usually come into

flower in one grand rush, and it is almost an impossibility to identify them as they develop. Collecting plants during the daylight hours of summer, putting them in the press in the evening, then identifying and mounting them in the winter is a rather common procedure among botanists.

(3) By collecting several plants of one species, it is possible to submit a duplicate to an expert for identification or confirmation. Almost any of these "authorities" are willing to do this with reasonable numbers; his payment is the plant specimen for his collection. Of course, make arrangements before sending the specimens.

2. *To identify other plants.*

(1) A set of named specimens will often aid in checking the identity of later material by allowing careful comparison. It is seldom possible to leaf through the collection and identify by general visual comparison only, especially in dealing with our particular group of plants that have a superficial similarity to each other. But it does often allow for checking a doubtful determination or helping decide between several possibilities. The key and description of the plant ought to have the final word of course.

(2) It goes without saying that your initial collection must be correctly named. There is something "final" and "sacred looking" about a name on a specimen, and mistakes in identification have a way of perpetuating themselves down through the years.

3. *Provides voucher specimens.*

(1) Research material ought to be substantiated with permanent specimens. Such lines of research as chromosome counts, physiological experiments, morphological observations, etc. should always also have on file pressed material of the plant used in the experiment.

(2) All records of plant distribution should be backed up by herbarium specimens. If anyone has a question about the plants, he can always refer to these. Every printed list of plants ought to be supported in this concrete fashion.

(3) Host plants for other organisms such as fungi and in-

sects should be on file in some herbarium. This is important in such studies as those on rusts and smuts, especially where the "Host Index" method of identifying these diseases is used.

GENERAL DIRECTIONS FOR COLLECTING

1. *Average specimen.* Select an average plant or collect several showing the range of variation. Remember your plant is to be a representative of the species for the area. There is a temptation to take an unusual (or even an abnormal) plant, but if you do this for any special reason, the entire situation should be clearly stated on the label.

2. *Fruit mature.* The ideal time to secure these plants is to wait until the fruits are just beginning to fall. The staminate parts may be incomplete by then, but this can usually be handled in various ways. Due to force of circumstances, very often it is necessary to collect the plant in less than ideal condition.

3. *Underground parts.* The roots themselves are seldom used in identification, but the presence of bulbs, corms, and rhizomes ought to be clearly shown on the specimen. Whether the plant is an annual or perennial should also be indicated. This sometimes means pressing only selected portions of the plant.

4. *Place in press soon.* This is particularly important in arid regions. It is practically impossible to make a good specimen from a badly wilted plant. Fortunately, grasses and grasslike plants are much better to deal with in this respect than are plants in general.

5. *Field book.* Most professional plant collectors give every plant collection a number, these numbers running consecutively throughout their own lifetime. The individual folder containing the plant need bear only a number through

the pressing process. The important data are kept in a permanent field book that is later used to make up the label. The only danger is the chance of the field book being lost or destroyed. The advantage is saving the labor of writing out duplication information; the collection can subsequently be cited by naming the collector and his number for the specimen.

INFORMATION FOR THE LABEL

1. *Habitat.* This is the local condition under which the plant grew, such as "growing in wet soil at the borders of a pond." In mountainous areas, the elevation of the collection is important. In this country, this is usually stated in feet above sea level.

2. *Locality.* This should be stated so that anyone not familiar with the local geography can still locate, at least approximately, the area from which the plant was secured. Most collectors refer to the direction and miles distant from some recorded town, with the county and state given.

Even when the town has ceased to exist, it will still be recorded on the older maps. Roads and route numbers have a way of changing through the years! Very local names such as "Jones Ranch" or "Paradise Valley" should not be used, at least not by themselves. It takes a little imagination to make a good label; that is, the ability to imagine yourself in the mental position of a complete stranger!

3. *Underground parts.* These parts should be completely represented, if at all possible, on the specimen, but the situation may well be stated also on the label. Sometimes, the rhizomes may break off from the specimen, for example, and it may be valuable to someone consulting it later, to have this information from the collector.

4. *Habit.* In general, this includes any characteristic about the plant that may aid in the understanding or identification of it, but does not happen to show on the specimen. This may

include such information as height of plant (especially if it is not indicated), type of branching, the angle of the culms in relation to the ground surface, etc. Again, this takes a little imagination (and experience) to figure out just what should be included. Labels do have to be kept fairly brief.

5. *Time of collection.* The day, month, and year of collection should be given. Many workers feel that this should be written out like "August 4, 1969" instead of "8/4/69" for the sake of absolute clarity. (8/4/69 might also mean April 8, 1869 to some people.)

6. *Collector.* The collector's name should be listed in such a manner that no confusion will result. The initials of the given name are important in many cases.

7. *Special information.* This may include almost anything of particular interest to the collector. Some of these things we have noticed on labels are soil type, ecological formation, economic importance, relative abundance, field variation, insect visitors, etc. If your plants are to be deposited in some specific herbarium, then it would be wise to write to the curator for his particular suggestions for collecting and recording information. This ought to be done well ahead of time.

EQUIPMENT FOR COLLECTING

1. *Collecting tool.* The majority of collectors of our plants use some type of geological pick for prying the plants out of the ground. This saves injury to the hand knuckles, especially in areas with rocks or spiny plants like cacti! A good knife also comes in very handy. (Figure 5-1.)

2. *Container for storage.* This may be

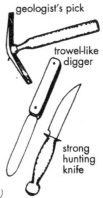

COLLECTING TOOLS *(Fig. 5-1)*

a lard can, a vasculum (collecting can), or one or more plastic bags. These prevent the plants from withering up from loss of moisture. This is especially important in arid regions. (Figure 5-2.)

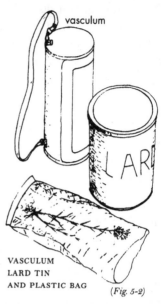

vasculum

VASCULUM
LARD TIN
AND PLASTIC BAG

(Fig. 5-2)

3. *Hand press.* This is made up of two stiff covers like wallboard with many single sheets of paper between. All this is bound by straps, usually with a handle for convenience for carrying it. The plants are placed in this temporary press as collected and actually begin the pressing process before being transferred to the regular press in the evening. (Figure 5-3.)

HAND PRESS *(Fig. 5-3)*

4. *Press.* This varies with the collector but usually consists of blotters and folded sheets of newspaper. The whole is bound by straps and boards and is expandable and transportable. (Figure 5-4.)

PLANT PRESS *(Fig. 5-4)*

SPECIAL DIRECTIONS FOR PRESSING

Here are some suggestions, particularly for handling specimens of grasses and grasslike plants. General suggestions can be found in Chapter XIII of *How to Identify Plants.*

1. *Number each.* Give every folder a number and have the duplicate plant sheets show the same one. Record all information in the field book.

2. *Make specimens.* Sort out as many individual specimens of each collection as you desire, making sure that each one has the required structures present.

3. *Arrange plant.* Place the specimen in the individual folder. This usually means folding it at least once. Our special groups of plants do not stay bent very well so that many collectors use prepared strips of cardboard to help hold them in place, or tear the newspaper folder as shown. (Figure 5-5.)

GRASS WITH
CARDBOARD STRIPS
AND NEWSPAPER
FOLDER
(Fig. 5-5)

4. *Blotters and press.* Place the folders with their enclosed specimens between thick blotters of about the same size (about 12″ x 18″). If blotters are not available, you can use several thicknesses of folded newspaper as a substitute for each. A board can be placed on top of the pile with a weight placed on top. A more conventional plant press is made up of two boards, these often latticed and slightly flexible, with ropes or straps placed around them. This unit can be readily transported. (Figure 5-6.)

5. *Change blotters.* Replace these blotters with dry ones as needed. The moist ones

PLANT PRESS *(Fig. 5-6)*

can be dried out and used again later. A good rule is to change blotters every twenty-four hours for several times; then change them as needed until the plant is pressed flat and is perfectly dry. This process varies with the relative succulence of the plant; fortunately, the grasses and their relatives are usually relatively easy to dry out in the press.

If you are in a hurry and wish to save blotter changing, or the air is humid and moist in the area, you may wish to use some form of artificial heat to dry out the specimens. Corrugated paper cardboards (or aluminum corrugates sold by supply houses) are inserted among the sheets, and the press is suspended above a heat source. This heat must not be too intense; you don't want the plants to scorch! Many collectors have a special box constructed that contains a heating unit and fan at the base. (Figure 5-7.)

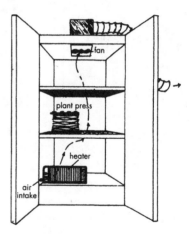

PLANT DRIER
(*Fig. 5-7*)

6. *Mount.* Fasten the dry plants to thin cardboards 11½ x 16½ inches in size. Thin paper does not hold its shape well, but very stiff, thick cardboard is unnecessary. These sheets can be purchased from biological supply houses. Glue the plants to the sheets or fasten them down with strips of gummed paper or cloth (or both). Tin paste or ordinary glue can be used in this process. Recently liquid plastic has been used by many botanists to hold down the specimens to the cardboard. This prepared material can be purchased already

made up. The strips are placed so as to prevent longitudinal slipping of the specimen, and enough space is left on the sheet for the label.

7. *Attach label.* This conventionally goes in the lower right hand corner. It is usually about 3″ x 4½″ in size. Space should be available for the information needed. These labels can be printed up to order or purchased from supply houses. (Figure 5-8.)

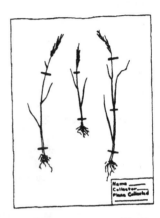

MOUNTED GRASS WITH LABEL
(*Fig. 5-8*)

8. *Store.* Store the specimens so that they are readily accessible. The usual custom is to file the plant sheets in genus covers, and these are placed in cabinets and cases. The damage caused by insects feeding on the dried plant material (sometimes actually breeding and multiplying in the cases) is fortunately seldom much of a problem in this group of plants.

Differences Between Grasses (Gramineae) and Sedges (Cyperaceae)

Character	Gramineae	Cyperaceae
Number of bracts closely associate with each flower	Two (lemma and palea) bracts, one (palea) 2-nerved	One bract (scale) all with odd number nerves
Second bract (perigynium), when present, surrounds flower	No	Yes
Spikelet (unit with glumes and floret or florets) present	Yes	No (flowers are in spikes)
Imperfect flowers present	Rare	Common
Fruit (ripened ovary)	Caryopsis	Achene
Embryo	Lateral to the endosperm	Embedded in the endosperm
Number of stigmas	Two	Two or three
Shape of culm (in cross-section)	Round	Triangular (esp. below infl.)
Center of culm	Hollow	Solid
Rank of leaves on the culm	Two	Three
Sheath of leaves	Open	Closed
Ligule	Definite	Absent or Indefinite

The word "*usually*" is understood in most of the above items.

VI

Sedges (*Cyperaceae*)

The same person who has made up his mind that grasses are very difficult to identify is pretty apt to consider the sedges to be almost impossible! Actually, neither idea will prove to be correct. While sedges have a host of new concepts that must be mastered before they can be handled in the treatments, some of the most common ones are presented in this chapter. Most of the difficulty occurs in checking the species of *Carex*. This genus is usually the largest in the entire area and creates a problem because of the sheer weight of number of species. Given a reasonable amount of study and practice, you will find that the sedges will prove to be moderately workable.

The differences between the grasses and the sedges are listed in the chart on the previous page. The word *usually* must be understood in most of these items. Further reading in this chapter may help to explain some of these characters.

VEGETATIVE TERMS

1. *Aphyllopodic.* The lower leaves of the culm are reduced to bladeless sheaths (compare *phyllopodic*). (Figure 6-1.)

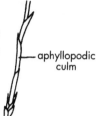

APHYLLOPODIC *(Fig. 6-1)*

2. *Phyllopodic.* The lower leaves of the stem with well-developed blades (compare *aphyllopodic*). (Figure 6-2.)

PHYLLOPODIC *(Fig. 6-2)*

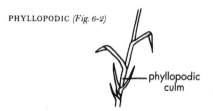

3. *Rhizomes present.* Prostrate and more or less underground stems growing partly or completely beneath the surface of the ground. (Figure 6-3.)

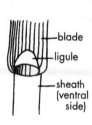

RHIZOMES PRESENT *(Fig. 6-3)*

4. *Annual and perennial.* The same concept discussed in Chapter I applies to sedges as well as grasses.

PARTS OF LEAF *(Fig. 6-4)*

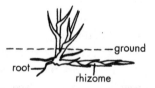

5. *Leaf parts.* The leaf is divided into blade and sheath (the latter closed unless torn). A *ligule* may be ascertained but is seldom used. (Figure 6-4.)

6. *Blades septate-nodulose.* The large longitudinal nerves bearing short lateral veins at intervals, these appearing to be more or less raised. (Figure 6-5.)

LEAF SEPTATE-NODULOSE *(Fig. 6-5)*

7. *Leaf sheath filamentose.* The sheaths, especially near the base of the culms of some sedges, fray out the longitudinal nerves by the disintegration of the tissue between. (Figure 6-6.)

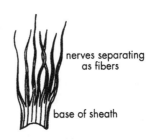

nerves separating as fibers

base of sheath

LEAF SHEATH FILAMENTOSE *(Fig. 6-6)*

8. *Leaf blades in section.* The commonest terms for the condition in cross-section are figured below. The term "involute" is loosely used for any tightly rolled leaf. (Figure 6-7.)

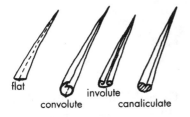

flat
convolute
involute
canaliculate

LEAF BLADES
IN SECTION
(Fig. 6-7)

FLOWER TERMS

1. *Perfect flower.* The perfect flower is reduced to a one-celled, one-seeded ovary, usually three stamens and usually numerous bristles thought to be remnants of a perianth. (Figure 6-8.)

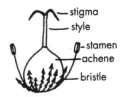

stigma
style
stamen
achene
bristle

PERFECT FLOWER *(Fig. 6-8)*

2. Bristles long or short.
Sometimes these bristles are comparatively short, sometimes they are long, even giving the whole spike a cottony appearance. (Figure 6-9.)

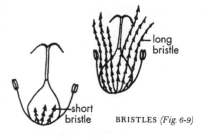

BRISTLES *(Fig. 6-9)*

3. Texture of style. Sometimes the texture of the style is relatively hard and rather shiny, resembling that of the achene. Other times the texture is more like that of the stigma, more fragile and darker in color. (Figure 6-10.)

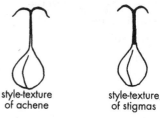

style-texture of achene

style-texture of stigmas

TEXTURE OF STYLE *(Fig. 6-10)*

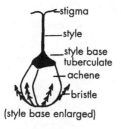

stigma

style

style base tuberculate

achene

bristle

(style base enlarged)

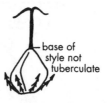

base of style not tuberculate

STYLE BASE TUBERCULATE *(Fig. 6-11)*

4. Style base tuberculate. The base of the style may enlarge (often called "biscuit-shaped") but may be of varying shape. This enlargement has a different texture from that of the achene which may project somewhat at the apex as shown. (Figure 6-11.)

trigonous (3-angled triangular)

lenticular

triquetrous

terete

ACHENE SHAPES IN SECTION *(Fig. 6-12)*

54

5. Achene shape in section. Some of the common shapes in cross-section are illustrated. (Figure 6-12.)

SCALES

The bract immediately subtending the perfect flower in sedges is called a "scale."

1. *Scales spirally arranged.* This is the common situation in sedges. You will note that they are in more than two ranks. (Figure 6-13.)

SCALES SPIRALLY ARRANGED *(Fig. 6-13)*

(more than 2-ranked)

2. *Scales two-ranked.* Less commonly the scales are inserted in two opposite rows on the rachis, making them two-ranked. (Figure 6-14.)

SCALES 2-RANKED *(Fig. 6-14)*

3. *Apex of scale.* The tip may vary from broadly rounded to awned. (Figure 6-15.)

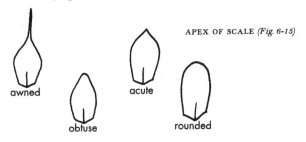

APEX OF SCALE *(Fig. 6-15)*

awned

obtuse

acute

rounded

INFLORESCENCE

The scales (with their subtending flowers) are crowded into units called "spikes" (or sometimes "spikelets," especially when they are small in size). These spikes may be one or more than one to a culm.

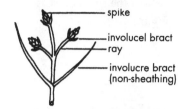

1. *Accessory parts.* These spikes may have accessory structures below them that have been given special terms. (Figure 6-16.)

2. *Bract sheathing.* Occasionally these bracts may be sheathing for a ways at the base, and this may be used to distinguish them from the non-sheathing bracts pictured in Figure 6-16. (Figure 6-17.)

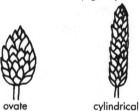

BRACT SHEATHING *(Fig. 6-17)*

3. *Shape of spike.* The individual spikes may have a characteristic shape that may be used in identification. Two common ones are pictured here. (Figure 6-18.)

SHAPE OF SPIKE *(Fig. 6-18)*

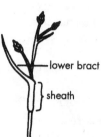

4. *Rachilla.* The axis on which the scales and flower are crowded (to form the spike) is called the rachilla. (Figure 6-19.)

RACHILLA *(Fig. 6-19)*

5. *Spikes remote.* When two or more spikes are present, they may be *remote* from each other. (Figure 6-20.)

6. *Spikes contiguous.* The spikes may be crowded to-

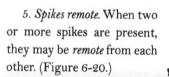

SPIKES REMOTE *(Fig. 6-20)*

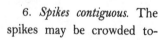

gether. See paragraphs 8 and 9 below. (Figure 6-21.)

SPIKES CONTIGUOUS AND SESSILE *(Fig. 6-21)*

7. *Spikes moniliform.* Sometimes the spikes are remote in characteristic beadlike fashion. (Figure 6-22.)

SPIKES MONILIFORM *(Fig. 6-22)*

8. *Spikes crowded and indistinguishable.* The spikes may be so crowded that it is hard to distinguish the individual ones without dissection. (Figure 6-23.)

SPIKES CROWDED AND
INDISTINGUISHABLE
(Fig. 6-23)

9. *Spikes crowded but distinguishable.* The spikes may be crowded but by looking closely one can make out the individual ones. (Figure 6-24.)

SPIKES CROWDED BUT DISTINGUISHABLE *(Fig. 6-24)*

II. Carex—Special Terms

The genus *Carex* is so different from the rest of the *Cyperaceae* that it is convenient to treat some of its concepts separately. This is done below.

GENERAL TERMS

1. *Flower.* The flowers are imperfect, staminate and pistillate, crowded closely on a short or long rachis in various arrangements. (See Figures 6-25 and 6-26.)

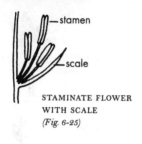

STAMINATE FLOWER
WITH SCALE
(Fig. 6-25)

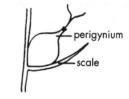

PISTILLATE FLOWER WITH SCALE
AND PERIGYNIUM (2 BRACTS)
(Fig. 6-26)

2. *Staminate.* The staminate flower is simple, being a cluster of usually three stamens. This flower is in the axis of a specialized bract called a "scale." (Figure 6-25.)

3. *Pistillate.* The pistillate flower is a bit more complicated, the pistil being surrounded completely by a specialized bract called a "perigynium." (Figure 6-26.) This perigynium is so modified and characteristic that it is discussed separately in a special treatment later on. (See also Figure 6-33.) (Figure 6-26.)

4. *Spike.* These flowers are crowded on the rachilla of one or more "spikes" (often called "spikelets"). The figure shows a solitary spike. (Figure 6-27.)

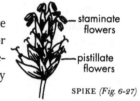

SPIKE *(Fig. 6-27)*

5. *Spikes staminate and pistillate.* The two types of flowers may be on different spikes. If the anthers are gone, the staminate spike can be located because it stays thin and undeveloped (it matures no achenes). (Figure 6-28.)

6. *Spikes androgynous.* Here the flowers are on the same spike, the staminate above, the pistillate below. The position of the staminate flower can be located in several ways. (1) The anthers may be present. (2) If these are lacking, the

SPIKES STAMINATE
AND PISTILLATE
(Fig. 6-28)

pale colored filaments may remain
(these are different from the stigmas of the pistillate flowers). (3)
The staminate portion of the spike
remains undeveloped and slim (as
described in 5 above). (Figure 6-29.)

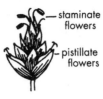

ANDROGYNOUS SPIKE
(Fig. 6-29)

7. *Spikes gynaecandrous.* The pistillate flowers may be above and the
staminate below on the same spike.
Read over numbers 5 and 6 again as
to how to tell the position of each.
(Figure 6-30.)

GYNAECANDROUS SPIKE
(Fig. 6-30)

8. *Scales relatively short.* This
is a concept that is difficult for
the beginner to visualize. The
scales are shorter and narrower
(especially above) than their
perigynia, exposing their tips
and edges when viewed from directly in front. Compare para-
graph 9 below. (Figure 6-31.)

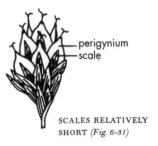

SCALES RELATIVELY
SHORT *(Fig. 6-31)*

9. *Scales relatively long.* The
scales may be so long and wide that
they conceal or nearly conceal their
perigynia which lie directly below.
(Figure 6-32.)

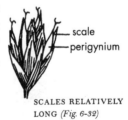

SCALES RELATIVELY
LONG *(Fig. 6-32)*

PERIGYNIUM TERMS

This is a characteristic bract that completely surrounds
the pistil in *Carex*. It is open only at or near the apex where
the stigma protrudes in flower. The perigynium is variable
and much used in classification. Some of the common con-

cepts are outlined here. They are applicable to a rather mature perigynium.

1. *Parts.* In the figure all the parts are present. The achene is shown inside by a dotted line. The *beak* and *stipe* may be lacking on some perigynia, and the stigmas may be broken off. (Figure 6-33.)

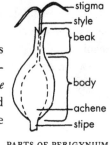

PARTS OF PERIGYNIUM
(Fig. 6-33)

2. *Shape.* The shape (as viewed from the side) is characteristic. Following are some common ones. (Figure 6-34.)

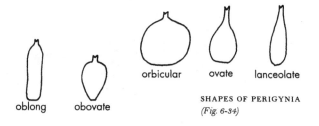

orbicular   ovate   lanceolate

oblong   obovate

SHAPES OF PERIGYNIA
(Fig. 6-34)

3. *Shape in section.* The shape in cross-section is characteristic. (Figure 6-35.)

PERIGYNIA SHAPE
(IN SECTION)
(Fig. 6-35)

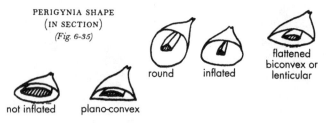

round   inflated   flattened biconvex or lenticular

not inflated   plano-convex

4. *Winged or wingless.* The edges may be wingless to broadly winged. (Figure 6-36.)

5. *Faces.* The faces of the perigynium are called "dorsal"

PERIGYNIA WINGED TO WINGLESS *(Fig. 6-36)*

wingless (2 keels) — keel

wing-margined

narrowly winged — wings

broadly winged

(the outer) and "ventral" (the inner). They may be similar in surface markings or much different. (Figure 6-37.)

6. *Nerves.* These are often listed as "finely nerved" and "coarsely nerved." (Figure 6-38.)

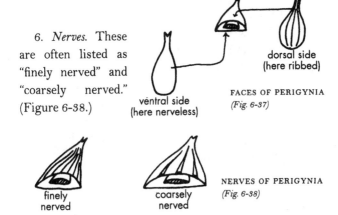

ventral side (here nerveless)

dorsal side (here ribbed)

FACES OF PERIGYNIA *(Fig. 6-37)*

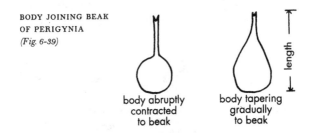

finely nerved

coarsely nerved

NERVES OF PERIGYNIA *(Fig. 6-38)*

7. *Body joining beak.* The body may taper up gradually into the beak or be abruptly contracted into it with intergradation between. The length of the perigynium is figured from the end of the beak to the base, unless otherwise stated. (Figure 6-39.)

BODY JOINING BEAK OF PERIGYNIA *(Fig. 6-39)*

body abruptly contracted to beak

body tapering gradually to beak

length

61

8. *Without a beak.* As suggested before, the beak of the perigynium may be lacking entirely. In such a case it may look something like the figure. (Figure 6-40.)

PERIGYNIUM WITHOUT BEAK *(Fig. 6-40)*

9. *Beak types.* The beaks of the perigynia may be of various types, some of which are figured. (Figure 6-41.)

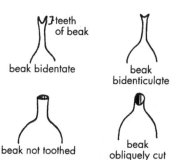

beak bidentate

beak bidenticulate

beak not toothed

beak obliquely cut

PERIGYNIA BEAK TYPES *(Fig. 6-41)*

10. *Beak shape in section.* The beaks may be round, flattened, or winged. (Figure 6-42.)

beak rounded

beak flattened

flattened and winged

BEAK SHAPE OF PERIGYNIA (IN SECTION) *(Fig. 6-42)*

11. *Ascending to reflexed.* The perigynium (and scales) may be ascending to reflexed on the rachilla. (Figure 6-43.)

PERIGYNIA ASCENDING, SPREADING, OR REFLEXED *(Fig. 6-43)*

scales and perigynia ascending

scales spreading (divergent)

lower scales reflexed (squarrose)

12. *How to tell number of stigmas.* There are at least two ways to ascertain this number.

A. You can count them, of course. But it is remarkable how often one or more stigmas have been broken off in the mature perigynia. One may find unbroken stigmas in protected areas such as in the axis of the spike and its rachis.

B. Judge by the shape of the achene and perigynium. This usually gives a good idea of the number of stigmas.

   (1) Achenes three-angled in section; perigynium round or roundish in section = *three stigmas.*

   (2) Achenes two-angled or flattened in section; perigynium flattened in section = *two stigmas.* (Figure 6-44.)

 — three stigmas

 — two stigmas

HOW TO TELL NUMBER OF STIGMAS IF THEY ARE ALL BROKEN OFF
(Fig. 6-44)

SOURCES FOR IDENTIFYING SEDGES

The general manuals and floras for identifying plants are usually used to check sedges. These are listed in Chapter VIII under "general floras." In addition we have local treatments available on the group, usually treating the species of a state or group of states. In general they are apt to be easier to use than the treatments covering a wider area since they contain fewer entities. The keys are short and ought to be easier to work. Of course, these local lists may be incomplete and may not contain sedges that represent recent introductions or those whose distribution were not known at the time. They include keys to the species and usually illustrations.

A notable example is Hermann's *Manual of the Carices of the Rocky Mountains and Colorado Basin* issued in 1970 as Agricultural Handbook No. 374 by the U.S.D.A. Anyone interested in sedges should investigate these local aids covering the areas where he is working. The following sources remain standard for North American sedges, although slightly out-of-date as to nomenclature.

1. Hermann, Frederick J. 1974. *Manual of the Genus Carex in Mexico and Central America.* U.S.D.A. Agri. Handb. No. 467.

2. Mackenzie, K. K. 1931–1935. Monograph of the *Cariceae. North American Flora.* Vol. 18 (1–7): 1–478. This work contains complete keys and descriptions to the species of the genus *Carex*, but no illustrations.

3. Mackenzie, K. K. 1940. *North American Cariceae.* 2 vols. New York Botanical Garden: New York. This follows the nomenclature of number two and contains an illustration of each species, and with shorter but still adequate descriptions.

4. Beetle, A. A. 1947. (Cyperaceae) Scirpeae (pars) *North American Flora* 18(8): 481-504.

5. Svenson, H. K. 1957. (Cyperaceae) Scirpeae *North American Flora* 18 (9); 505–556.

SUMMARY

Sedges (Cyperaceae)
(Fig. 44-1 to 44-9)

1. Perfect flower on rachis of spike. (Only one flower shown.) These are crowded as in No. 2.

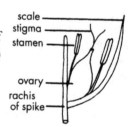

scale
stigma
stamen

ovary
rachis
of spike

Fig. 6-44 (1)

2. Spike or spikelet of flowers, each subtended by a scale (scales two-ranked here). These spikes single on the culm or as in No. 3.

Fig. 6-44 (2)

3. Group of three spikes.

Fig. 6-44 (3)

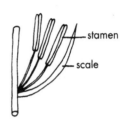

4. Staminate flower with scale.

Fig. 6-44 (4)

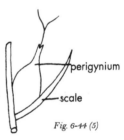

5. Pistillate flower with scale and perigynium (two bracts). See No. 6.

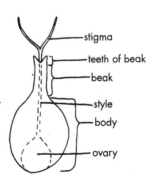

Fig. 6-44 (5)

6. Perigynium with pistillate flower inside.

Fig. 6-44 (6)

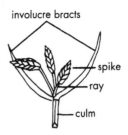

7. Staminate and pistillate flowers on completely separate spikes.

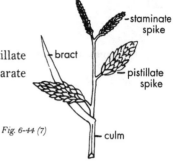

Fig. 6-44 (7)

8. On same spike, the staminate above, the pistillate below. Androgynous.

Fig. 6-44 (8)

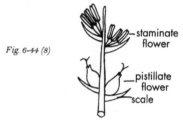

9. On same spike, the staminate below, the pistillate above. Gynaecandrous.

Fig. 6-44 (9)

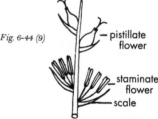

GENERAL SUGGESTIONS FOR IDENTIFYING SEDGES

1. *Collect the underground parts.* You will have to make such decisions as to "annual or perennial, presence or absence of rhizomes, caespitose culms or not, aphyllopodic or phyllopodic," and the complete plant will be needed.

2. *Be sure the perigynia are mature in Carex.* The descriptions of this structure apply to a reasonably mature one. If they are too ripe, they lose their stigmas and finally shatter off the spike.

3. *Read over Chapter IX.* The suggestions for identifying grasses usually apply equally well to sedges.

4. *Be patient until the terms are understood.* Here is when the going is slow and hard. Later on things always get easier.

VII

Rushes (*Juncaceae*)

The rushes are treated here because they are somewhat grasslike in general appearance. You will soon observe that this resemblance is largely superficial and the floral characters are much different. A grass-looking plant that does not have the right floral characters for a grass or sedge is almost sure to be a rush. That includes a capsule with few to many seeds, three to six stamens, and a dry, regular perianth in more or less two definite sets (these may be called sepals and petals). As you will recall, this differs from the floral set-up of the sedges and grasses. However, many of the concepts on the vegetative structure of these plants apply equally well to rushes.

FLOWER AND INFLORESCENCES

1. *Flower.* (Figure 7-1.)

FLOWER
(Fig. 7-1)

pistil

stamen

outer perianth

inner perianth

2. *Floral diagram.*
(Figure 7-2.)

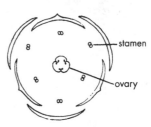

FLORAL DIAGRAM
(Fig. 7-2)

3. *Typical Inflorescence.*
(Figure 7-3.)

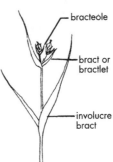

TYPICAL INFLORESCENCE
(Fig. 7-3)

4. *Headlike Inflorescence.*
(Figure 7-4.)

HEADLIKE INFLORESCENCE
(Fig. 7-4)

CAPSULES

1. *Capsule three-celled.* (Figure 7-5.)

CAPSULE THREE-CELLED
(Fig. 7-5)

2. *Capsule one-celled.*
(Figure 7-6.)

CAPSULE
ONE-CELLED
(Fig. 7-6)

capsule round
in cross section

capsule trigonous
in cross section

69

3. *Capsule shape.* (Figure 7-7a; Figure 7-7b.)

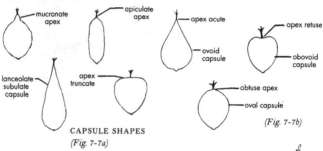

CAPSULE SHAPES
(Fig. 7-7a)

(Fig. 7-7b)

SEEDS

1. *Caudate.* (Figure 7-8.)

SEED NOT
CAUDATE
(Fig. 7-8)

SEED
CAUDATE
(TAILED)

2. *Seeds with white strophiole-like bases.*
(Figure 7-9.)

SEEDS WITH WHITE
STROPHIOLE-LIKE BASES
(Fig. 7-9)

LEAVES

1. *Lower bract terete, resembling culms.*
(Figure 7-10.)

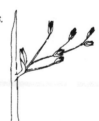

LOWER BRACT TERETE,
RESEMBLING CULMS
(Fig. 7-10)

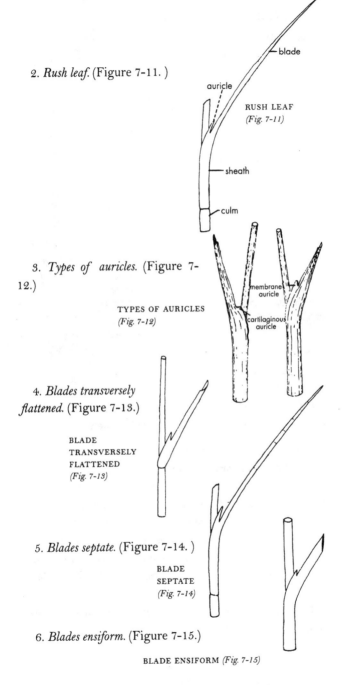

2. *Rush leaf.* (Figure 7-11.)

RUSH LEAF
(Fig. 7-11)

blade

auricle

sheath

culm

3. *Types of auricles.* (Figure 7-12.)

TYPES OF AURICLES
(Fig. 7-12)

membrane
auricle

cartilaginous
auricle

4. *Blades transversely flattened.* (Figure 7-13.)

BLADE
TRANSVERSELY
FLATTENED
(Fig. 7-13)

5. *Blades septate.* (Figure 7-14.)

BLADE
SEPTATE
(Fig. 7-14)

6. *Blades ensiform.* (Figure 7-15.)

BLADE ENSIFORM *(Fig. 7-15)*

71

7. *Blades terete.*
(Figure 7-16.)

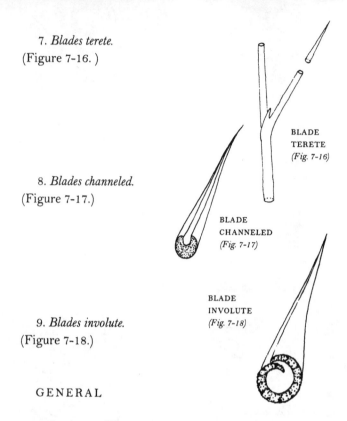

BLADE
TERETE
(Fig. 7-16)

8. *Blades channeled.*
(Figure 7-17.)

BLADE
CHANNELED
(Fig. 7-17)

BLADE
INVOLUTE
(Fig. 7-18)

9. *Blades involute.*
(Figure 7-18.)

GENERAL

1. Read over Chapter IX on "Suggestions for Identifying Grasses." Many of the hints are applicable here.

2. There are few bulletins dealing exclusively with the rushes of a particular area. Consequently the list of General Manuals for Identification of Plants given in Chapter VIII must be used to find a treatment of this group of plants. Fortunately, there will usually be found comparatively few species in the area covered by these general treatments.

One that deserves special mention is Frederick J. Hermann's *Manual of the Rushes (Juncus spp.) of the Rocky Mountains and Colorado Basin.* General Technical Report RM-18. Rocky Mountain Forest and Range Experiment Station, U.S.D.A. Forest Service, 1975.

VIII

Manuals and Floras

A manual or flora that can be used to identify grasses has been written for almost every part of North America. Some of them are rather old, many are now out of print. They can usually be obtained from libraries or by purchase from dealers in secondhand books. Recently, several of these have been reprinted as individually noted.

Only the most important, often recently published, manuals or floras are listed in this chapter,* and only those limited to the United States, including Alaska, Hawaii, and Canada. I have given only regional, general publications unless the local area is inadequately treated. In a few cases, nearby areas are also included. If you wish to identify a grass from other places of the world, consult the following:

1. Blake, S. F. and A. Atwood. 1942. *Geographical Guide to Floras of the World.* Washington, D.C.: U.S.D.A. Misc. Pub. No. 401.

2. S. F. Blake. 1961. *Geographical Guide to Floras of the World.* Washington, D.C.: U.S.D.A. Misc. Pub. No. 797.

*Manuals relative to Sedges and Rushes are listed in their respective chapters.

3. ————. 1954. *Guide to Popular Floras of the United States and Alaska.* Washington, D.C.: U.S.D.A. Bibliographical Bull. No. 23.

4. Core, E. L. 1955. *Plant Taxonomy.* New York: Prentice-Hall. Chapter XI deals with the literature of Systematic Botany.

5. Lawrence, G. H. M. 1951. *Taxonomy of the Vascular Plants.* New York: MacMillan. Chapter XIV deals with the literature of Systematic Botany and gives the more important manuals and floras of the world's continents and islands.

Many of these so-called "popular" floras are based on long and careful study of the plants of the area covered. They are often short and may contain only the "common" species; also the grasses may be rather neglected. However, they can be very handy, especially in providing a list of the grasses likely to be encountered in a limited area.

GENERAL TREATMENTS OF GRASSES

These books are valuable in providing the background information so necessary in identifying grasses. Usually they do not provide usable keys for this identification.

1. Arber, Agnes. 1934. *The Gramineae.* Cambridge: Cambridge University Press. Reprinted in 1965 by Stechert-Hafner Service Agency.

2. Booth, W. E. 1964. *Agrostology.* Bozeman, Montana: The Endowment and Research Foundation at Montana State College.

3. Chase, Agnes. 1973. *First Book of Grasses.* New York: MacMillan.

4. Gould, Frank W. 1968. *Grass Systematics.* New York: McGraw-Hill. A key to genera of the grasses of the United States is included.

5. Hitchcock, A. A. 1914. *Textbook of Grasses.* New York: MacMillan.

WORLD—FOR IDENTIFICATION
OF GRASSES

1. Bentham, G. and J. D. Hooker. 1862–1883. *Genera Plantarum*. 3 vols. London. In Latin. The grass genera are treated in their proper place.

2. Bews, J. W. 1929. *The World's Grasses*. London: Longmans, Green and Co. General treatment and key to genera.

3. Engler, A. and Prantl, K. 1887–1915. *Die Naturlichen Pflanzenfamilien*. 23 vols. Leipzig: W. Engelmann. Treats the plant families and genera of the world (except the Bacteria). Second edition in preparation.

CULTIVATED GRASSES
OF NORTH AMERICA

Many grasses have found their way into cultivation. Of course, any native grass may be used occasionally in ornamentation, and those may not appear in the following treatments.

1. Bailey, L. H. 1914–1917. *The Standard Cyclopedia of Horticulture*. 6 vols. New York: MacMillan. Re-issued in 1935 in 3 volumes.

2. ———. 1929. *Manual of Cultivated Plants*. 2nd ed. New York: MacMillan. Rev. ed. 1949. The cultivated grasses are keyed out in regular manual fashion; the work is smaller than the cyclopedia and easier to transport.

3. Rehder, A. 1960. *Manual of Cultivated Trees and Shrubs*. 2nd ed. New York: MacMillan. The few genera of woody grasses are listed in this work.

NORTH AMERICA (NOT USUALLY
INCLUDING THE U.S.) AND
SOUTHERN CANADA

1. Beal, W. J. 1887, 1896. *Grasses of North America*. 2 vols. New York: Henry Holt.

2. Britton, N. L. and C. F. Millspaugh. 1920. *The Bahama Flora.* New York: The Authors.

3. Britton, N. L. 1905. *North American Flora.* New York: New York Botanical Garden. 1905—Grasses by Nash and Hitchcock.

4. Hitchcock, A. S. 1909. *Catalogue of the Grasses of Cuba.* Contrib. U.S. Nat. Herb. 12. 6:183–256.

5. Hitchcock, A. S. 1913–1916. *Mexican Grasses in U.S.* Contrib. Nat. Herb. 17;3:181–387.

6. Hitchcock, A. S. 1930. *Grasses of Central America.* Contrib. U.S. Nat. Herb. 24;9:557.

7. Hitchcock, A. S. 1936. *Manual of the Grasses of West Indias.* U.S.D.A. Misc. Pub. No. 243.

8. Polunin, Nicholas. 1959. *Circumpolar Arctic Flora.* Oxford: Clarendon Press.

9. Standley, Paul C. 1930–1936. *Trees and Shrubs of Mexico.* Contrib. U.S. Nat. Herb. 4461, vol. 23, parts 1–5. Eight genera of woody grasses are given, including four bamboo genera.

WHOLE UNITED STATES—GRASSES ONLY (INCLUDING SOUTHERN CANADA)

1. Hitchcock, A. S. 1920. *Genera of Grasses of the United States.* U.S.D.A. Bul. 772.

2. Hitchcock, A. S. 1951. *Manual of Grasses of the United States.* U.S. Dept. of Agri. Misc. Pub. 200. Reprinted 1971 by Dover Publications.

3. Hitchcock, A. S. 1935. *Manual of Grasses of the United States.* U.S.D.A. Misc. Pub. 200.

4. Pohl, R. W. 1945. *How to Know the Grasses.* Dubuque, Iowa: W.C. Brown. Revised edition, 1968.

5. Vasey, G. 1883–1892. *The Grasses of the United States.* U.S.D.A. Special Report No. 63.

GRASSES ONLY—PORTIONS OF THE UNITED STATES (SOME OF THE OLDER LOCAL TREATMENTS ARE OMITTED.)

Alaska and Hawaii (grasses only)

1. Hitchcock, A. S. 1922. *The Grasses of Hawaii.* Honolulu: Mem. Bernice P. Bishop Museum. 8:101–230.

2. Hubbard, W. A. 1955. *Grasses of British Columbia.* Victoria, B.C.: Provincial Museum.

3. Lamson-Scribner, F. and Merril, E. D. 1910. *Grasses of Alaska.* Contrib. U.S. Nat. Herb. 13(3).

4. Rotar, P. 1968. *Grasses of Hawaii.* Honolulu: Univ. of Hawaii Press.

Northeastern United States (grasses only)

1. Core, E. L., E. E. Berkley, and H. A. Davis. 1944. *West Virginia Grasses.* West Virginia Agri. Expt. Sta. Bull. 313.

2. Deam, C. C. 1929. *Grasses of Indiana.* Indianapolis, Ind.: Wm. B. Burford.

3. Fassett, N. C. 1951. *Grasses of Wisconsin.* Madison: Univ. of Wisconsin Press.

4. Gress, E. M. 1924. *The Grasses of Pennsylvania.* Penn. Dept. Agri. Gen. Bul. 384.

5. Mohlenbrock, Robt. H. 1972. *The Illustrated Flora of Illinois Grasses.* Carbondale: Southern Illinois Univ. Press and Feffer and Simmons.

6. Mosher, E. 1918. *The Grasses of Illinois.* Univ. of Illinois Agri. Exp. Sta. Bul. 205.

7. Schaffner, J. H. 1949. *The Grasses of Ohio.* Columbus: Ohio State University.

Southeastern and Southcentral United States (grasses only)

1. Blomquist, H. L. 1948. *Grasses of North Carolina.* Durham, N. C.: Duke University Press.

2. Featherby, H. I. 1946. *Manual of Grasses of Oklahoma.* Stillwater: Oklahoma State Univ. Bul., vol. 43, no. 21.

3. Gould, Frank W. 1975. *The Grasses of Texas*. College Station: Texas A & M Univ. Press.

4. Silveus, W. A. 1933. *Texas Grasses*. San Antonio, Texas: The Author.

Midwest—West of Mississippi River, West to Rocky Mountains (grasses only)

1. Gates, F. C. 1936. *Grasses in Kansas*. Reports of the Kansas State Board of Agriculture, vol. IV, no. 220A.

2. Kucera, C. L. 1961. *The Grasses of Missouri*. Univ. of Missouri Studies 35.

3. Pammel, L. H., C. R. Ball, and F. Lamson-Scribner. 1905. *The Grasses of Iowa*. Iowa Geological Survey, Part II. (Part I is a general treatment of the subject.)

4. Wilcox, C. M., G. K. Link, and V. W. Pool. 1915. *A Handbook of Nebraska Grasses*. University of Agri. Experiment Station Bul. 148.

Western and Southwestern United States (grasses only)

1. Flowers, S. 1959. *Common Grasses of Utah*. 3rd ed. Salt Lake City: Univ. of Utah Press.

2. Gould, F. W. 1951. *Grasses of the Southwestern United States*. University of Arizona Biol. Sci. Bul. 7.

3. Porter, C. L. 1964. *A Flora of Wyoming, Part III*. Poaceae (Gramineae). Bul. 418. University of Wyoming Agri. Expt. Stat.

4. Vasey, G. 1891. *Grasses of the Southwest, in Illustrations of North American Grasses*, Parts I and II. U.S.D.A.

5. Vasey, G. 1893. *Grasses of the Pacific Slope, in Illustrations of North American Grasses*, Parts I and II. U.S.D.A.

GENERAL MANUALS (INCLUDING GRASSES) OF UNITED STATES AND SOUTHERN CANADA

Local treatments such as the floras of states are sometimes omitted here.

Alaska (general floras)

1. Anderson. J. P. 1959. *Flora of Alaska and Adjacent Parts of Canada.* Ames: Iowa University Press.

2. Hulten, E. 1941–1950. *Flora of Alaska and Yukon, Parts I–X.* Gloreup: Lunds Univ. arssk. Lund.

3. Hulten, E. 1960. *The Flora of the Aleutian Islands and Westernmost Alaska Peninsula, with Notes on the Flora of Commander Island.* New York: J. Cramer; New York: Hafner Publishing Co.

4. Polunin, Nicholas. 1959. *Circumpolar Arctic Flora.* Oxford: Clarendon Press.

5. Wiggans, I. L. and J. H. Thomas. 1962. *A Flora of the Alaskan Slope.* Arctic Inst. of North America. Sp. Pub. 4. Toronto: University of Toronto Press.

Hawaii (general floras)

1. Degener, Otto. 1933–1962. *Flora Hawaiiensis or the New Illustrated Flora of the Hawaiian Islands.* Honolulu. Book I–VII. (Incomplete.)

2. Hillebrand. W. 1888. *Flora of the Hawaiian Islands.* London and New York: The Author. Reprinted in 1965 by Hafner Publishing Co.

Canada (general floras; see also floras of Alaska and Northern United States whose range extends into adjacent Canada)

1. Louis-Marie, Pere. 1931. *Flore-manuel de la province de Quebec.* Montreal, Canada. Contrib. No. 23 Institut d'Okra.

2. Macoun, J. 1883–1902. *Catalogue of Canadian Plants.* Geol. and Nat. Hist. Survey of Canada, 7 parts. Montreal, Canada. (Additions to 1906.)

3. Marie-Victorin, Frere. 1947. *Flore laurentienne.* Montreal, Canada: Freres des ecoles chretiennes.

4. Moss, E. H. 1959. *Flora of Alberta.* Toronto: Univ. of Toronto Press.

5. Polunin, Nickolas. 1959. *Circumpolar Arctic Flora.* Oxford: Clarendon Press.

Northeastern United States (general floras)

1. Britton, N. L. and A. Brown. 1896. *An Illustrated Flora of the Northern United States and Canada.* 3 vols. New York: Scribner and Sons. 2nd ed. 1913. Reprinted in 1970 in 3 paperback volumes by Dover Publications.

2. Deam, W. B. 1940. *Flora of Indiana.* Indianapolis: Wm. B. Burford Printing Co.

3. Fernald, M. L. 1950. *Grays Manual of Botany.* 8th ed. New York: American Book Co.

4. Gleason, H. 1952. *The New Britton and Brown Illustrated Flora of the Northeastern United States and Adjacent Canada.* 3 vols. New York: New York Botanical Garden. This revised edition covers a more limited area.

5. Gleason, H. A. and A. Cronquist. 1963. *Manual of Vascular Plants of Northeastern United States and Adjacent Canada.* Princeton: Van Nostrand, Inc.

6. Jones, G. N. and G. D. Fuller. 1955. *Vascular Plants of Illinois.* Urbana: Univ. of Illinois Press.

7. Schaffner, J. H. 1928. *Field Manual of the Flora of Ohio and Adjacent Territory.* Columbus: R.G. Adams.

8. Seymour, F. C. 1969. *The Flora of New England.* Rutland, Vt.: Charles E. Tuttle Co.

Southeastern and Southcentral United States (general floras)

1. Correll, D. S. and M. C. Johnston. 1970. *Manual of the Vascular Plants of Texas.* Texas Research Foundation.

2. Long, R. W. and O. Lakela. 1971. *A Flora of Tropical Florida.* Coral Gables: Univ. of Miami Press.

3. Radford, A. E., H. E. Ahles, and C. R. Bell. 1964. *Guide to the Vascular Flora of the Carolinas.* The Book Exchange, Univ. of North Carolina.

4. Small, J. K. 1913. *Flora of the Southeastern United States.* New York: The Author. 2nd ed. This is the work on which the next revision was based. It is still rather important because it contains the *Pteridophyta* and extends further west in its official range.

5. Small, J. K. 1933. *Manual of the Southeastern Flora.* Chapel Hill: Univ. of North Carolina Press.

Midwestern United States (general floras)

1. Rydberg, P. A. 1932. *Flora of the Prairies and Plains of Central North America.* New York: New York Bot. Garden. Reprinted in 1971 in 2 paperback volumes by Dover Publications, New York.

2. Stevens, O. A. 1950. *Handbook of North Dakota Plants.* Fargo, N. D.: Knight Printing Co.

3. Steyermark, J. A. 1963. *Flora of Missouri.* Ames: Iowa State Univ. Press.

4. Winter, J. 1936. *An Analysis of the Flowering Plants of Nebraska.* Conservation Dept. Bull. No. 13. Conserv. and Survey Div., University of Nebraska.

Western United States (general floras)

1. Abrams, L. 1940–1960. *An Illustrated Flora of the Pacific States: Washington, Oregon and California.*

2. Coulter, J. and A. A. Nelson. 1909. *New Manual of Botany of Central Rocky Mountains.* New York: American Book Co.

3. Cronquist, A., A. H. Holmgren, N. H. Holmgren, and J. L. Reveal. 1972. *Intermountain Flora, Vascular Plants of the Intermountain West,* Vol I. New York: Hafter Publishing Co.

4. Davis, R. 1952. *Flora of Idaho.* Dubuque, Iowa: William C. Brown Co.

5. Harrington, H. D. 1954. *Manual of the Plants of Colorado.* Chicago: Swallow Press.

6. Hitchcock, C. L., A. Cronquist, M. Ownbey, and J. W. Thompson. 1955–1969. *Vascular Plants of the Pacific Northwest.* 5 vols. Seattle: Univ. of Washington Press.

7. Jepson, W. L. 1923–1925. *A Manual of the Flowering Plants of California.* Univ. of California.

8. Kearney, T. H. and R. H. Peebles. 1951. *Arizona Flora.* Berkeley: Univ. of California Press. 1960 printing contains supplement.

9. Munz, P. A. 1974. *A Flora of Southern California.* Berkeley: Univ. of California Press. (Supercedes the author's *A Manual of Southern California Botany.*)

10. Munz, P. A. (and D. D. Keck). 1959. *A California Flora.* Berkeley: Univ. of California Press.

11. Peck, M. E. 1941. *A Manual of the Higher Plants of Oregon.* Portland, Ore.: Binfords and Mort. 1961. 3rd. ed.

12. Rydberg, P. A. 1922. *Flora of the Rocky Mountains and Adjacent Plains.* 2nd ed. Published by The Author.

13. Tidestrom, I. 1925. *Flora of Utah and Nevada.* Contrib. U.S. Herb. Vol. 25.

14. Tidestrom, I., and Sister T. Kittell. 1941. *Flora of Arizona and New Mexico.* Washington, D.C.: Catholic Univ. Press.

15. Wooton, E. O. and P. C. Standley. 1915. *Flora of New Mexico.* Contrib. U.S. Nat. Herb. Vol. 19.

MONOGRAPHS OF GENERA OF GRASSES

These treat certain genera of grasses (rarely sections of), usually the large ones. They may include all the species of the world or of a more limited area. Usually they include more complete descriptions and distributional information than do the regional floras. However, since they seldom are available to the average student, they are not specifically listed here.

IX

Suggestions for Identifying Grasses

This chapter is designed to provide some practical help to the beginning student of grasses. However, it is in no sense a substitute for actual practice. Consider merely reading it over at first, then after some experience in identifying, come back to it and study it carefully. The suggestions should mean a lot more to you then. Above all, do not get discouraged when progress seems slow at first; it will be easier and quicker later on.

KEYS

1. Keys certainly provide a convenient short-cut method of identifying plants.

2. You must understand the vocabulary used. Technical terms are commonly used and are necessary. A simple, easy-to-use key may be fun to play with, but can never lead you to a correct identification of grasses of an area.

3. There is a "knack" in using a key. Some students pick it up more quickly than others. The first step is the correct di-

agnosis of the material. A good key will be of no value to you unless you have this correct understanding of the plant. Following is a set of 25 questions concerning a grass that may help, if you fill them out correctly. It is suggested you do this for a few grasses before you try identifying them. Perhaps you can have an expert check your answers. Or try it out on a grass you already know, like wheat, oats, or Kentucky bluegrass. Then you can key out the grass for practice and check your preliminary diagnosis with the recorded description.

Diagnosis Check

Write the word that answers the question in the blank space before the number. Words *in italics* are to be used in those answers.

Be sure your specimen is not abnormal or badly shattered. For number of parts of measurements, give the average of several determinations. Omit any question that does not apply.

_____ 1. Is the plant *annual* or *perennial?*

_____ 2. Are the rhizomes *present* or *absent?*

_____ 3. Is the ligule made up of *hairs* or a *membrane?*

_____ 4. Are auricles *present* or *absent?*

_____ 5. Are the leaf blades nearest *involute* or *flat?*

_____ 6. List the surface type for the leaf sheath (*glabrous, scabrous, pubescent, pilose,* etc.).

_____ 7. Are the sheaths *open* or *closed* (for half or more their length)?

_____ 8. Name the type of inflorescence (*spike, raceme, panicle*).

_____ 9. Is the inflorescence *open* or *contracted?*

_____ 10. Is the articulation *above* or *below* the glumes?

_____ 11. Is the spikelet *terete, laterally,* or *dorsally* compressed?

_____ 12. Is the sterile floret (or florets) *none, above,* or *below* the fertile?

_____ 13. Are the florets *bisexual* or *unisexual?*

_____ 14. How many florets to a spikelet? (Give average, counting reduced ones too.)

_____ 15. Are the glumes as *long, longer,* or *shorter* than the spikelet?

_____ 16. How many nerves to the first glume?

_____ 17. How many nerves to the second glume?

_____ 18. Give the average length of the lemma.

_____ 19. How many nerves are present on the lemma?

_____ 20. Are the nerves of the lemma *parallel* or *converging?*

_____ 21. Is the lemma *rounded* or *compressed keeled* on the back?

_____ 22. Is the lemma *awnless, dorsally,* or *terminally awned?*

_____ 23. Is the lemma either webbed or bearded at the base? (*Yes* or *No*)

_____ 24. List surface type for the lemma proper (*glabrous, scabrous, pubescent,* etc.).

_____ 25. Describe the texture of the lemma (*scarious, membranaceous, chartaceous, cartilaginous, coriaceous, indurate*).

Like the human beings that create them, identification keys may encompass errors and mistakes. It is easy to criticize them, as the author discovered in writing an article about key-making (1951. *Turtox News* 29 (9):166–168), but hard to construct a good workable one. The most reasonable way to proceed is to recognize that these faults and difficulties do exist and then work out good methods to deal with them. For that reason, these trouble-makers are listed here first, with suggestions given for handling them later on.

1. The key may sometimes use characters of the plant not indicated on your specimen. Examples of this could be the presence or absence of rhizomes, the type of articulation, the annual and perennial habit, and many others.

2. The key is likely to be set up for the average plant; your plant may be abnormal.

3. Technical terms may vary in their exact meaning among different authors. A few such terms are *caespitose*, *membranous*, *involute*, *tall*, and *short*. Fortunately, there are not too many of these, and one soon gets used to the author's treatment of these terms.

4. The characters used in the key may not contrast exactly, especially the secondary ones. An example would be:
1) lemmas membranaceous; plants annual   No. 1 species
2) lemmas indurate   No. 2 choice

The duration habit of the plants in the second choice can often be checked by reading further in the key. It probably contains both plants that are annual and perennial, but, if that is so, it really should be stated clearly, although very often that is not done.

5. Keys are in fine print, and it is easy to overlook a step. This is particularly apt to occur in a long key.

6. The key may contain major or minor mistakes.

Sometimes the exceptions to the general rule are not provided for in the key. For example, there may be one annual species within a large genus. The key-maker may forget about this and place the whole genus under "perennial" only.

There is a special "knack" in running keys as mentioned before, based on experience, partly on common sense. As a beginner you have to trust the treatment in general but still must consider the possibility that it may let you down on any particular point. When to "give in" on a character, when to "hew to the line" takes judgement. The key may actually be faulty on a point; on the other hand, you may be in the wrong place entirely, due to your own previous mistake!

7. The plant may not be included in the key. Perhaps it is a newly introduced weedy grass. When it will not run down nicely, you can often pick it up in some other treatment.

8. The illustrations, when present, do not show the range of variation of a species and should not be depended upon too much. In fact, these pictures may actually show an extreme and not the average. The descriptions should always have the last word.

9. There are a few frustrating genera that do not seem to fit anywhere and are sometimes ignored by the key. Examples would be *Buchloe, Hilaria, Cenchrus,* and *Coix.* Sometimes in identifying them you have to "cast around" a bit, but fortunately these unusual genera are easy to spot when you encounter them in the key.

HINTS ON USING KEYS

1. It is advisable that you look over the grass in a general way before starting to key it. It is usually not feasible to study every character carefully before you start the identification; some of them you may not actually need. However, in the flurry of making decisions, in using the key you may have overlooked some very obvious major character.

2. Check at every point with the recorded descriptions (of tribe, genus, and species). This may take you a bit longer but may prevent delaying mistakes.

3. Run the grass both ways in cases of doubt. For example, should the key choices be "annual" or "perennial" and you just cannot decide, you still have an excellent chance of identifying it. One way will read wrong (perhaps fitting neither possible alternatives) or arrive at an entity that simply will not fit the specimen at hand. But the correct route should fit smoothly and arrive finally at a more satisfactory place. Often, several of these trials can be made at different places in a long key, even if it all may get rather involved.

Some workers try both ways even when the first one sounds very attractive, just for the added certainty. It may be a good idea to try the short route first; perhaps it will fit so well that the long one can be ignored.

4. Learn to pick out and evaluate the important characters. In grasses, these will normally be the ones associated with the spikelet. For example, usually you would do well to give more weight to the length of the lemma than to the height of the culm.

5. Read all the supplementary characters given in the key even though the first one listed seems to provide reasonable certainty. This primary character is supposed to be the most important one, but it may not happen to be the most obvious one on your particular specimen. In any event, the secondary ones may be of value by adding cumulative evidence.

6. When illustrations are appended they can often be used to check on what is meant by certain visual characters in the key. For example, if "panicles condensed" is used in contrast to "panicles open," look forward to see what these look like, checking several pictorial representatives of each.

7. Use your previous knowledge of the group, but with caution. Be careful of preconceived notions that may be wrong. Such fixed ideas are attractive and are hard to give

up! If the grass will not key down, then turn back and check each character with an open mind—even the major ones!

8. Read both contrasting categories. Often the first one sounds so attractive that the second choice is ignored altogether. However, this alternative may actually help explain the first statement, if only by contrast.

9. In measuring a part, remember to select a rather large representative, although not an abnormally large one.

10. Check the plant by referring to its recorded habitat. For example, if you are identifying a specimen you found in very wet ground and you key it to a species that is described as "plants of dry rocky hillsides," then you have a right to suspect your identification. Of course, your manual could be wrong on the matter or have incomplete information.

11. Also, check the recorded locality. If the plant is not listed from your area or even near your state, then be careful! The same caution applies as for habitat; the last word often isn't all in on such matters, especially if the species is weedy and may have been recently spread around very rapidly.

X

Identification of Grasses
in Vegetative Condition

WHY THIS MAY BE NECESSARY

It sometimes becomes necessary to identify certain grasses before (or after) the flowering and fruiting structures are present. This requires special techniques and special treatments. A few situations in which this kind of identification may become very useful are listed below as samples.

1. Ecologists making quadrat studies may find many grasses in vegetative condition only, and need the names in order to list them for the record.

2. Studies in the grazing habits of various animals may need a tentative identification of certain common grasses in order to list them in their records.

3. General floral lists of an area, especially if made early in the season, may necessitate a similar procedure.

Most books and keys on this subject deal with the local grasses only, and contain relatively few species as compared to the total present. The ones included are apt to be the so-called "common" ones of the area, but of course these are apt to be just the ones encountered by someone. Vegetative keys are surprisingly easy to use and most students find that they work relatively rapidly. This may be due in part to the limited numbers of plants actually covered, but also because the necessary concepts are rather easy to acquire oneself or to explain to someone else. Absolute certainty as to the correct identification is another thing. It is usually wise to treat the name secured as a tentative one for purposes of record, to be checked upon later in the season when the grass heads out. In some cases there may be a modicum of truth in the statement sometimes made, "Why, even a wrong name may be better than no name at all!" If it can be checked and possibly corrected later on, then this actually may be true.

CHARACTER USED

1. *Annual or perennial.* This character is discussed for grasses in general in Chapter I, and the statements there with their accompanying drawings should be rechecked. This is a difficult concept for the beginning student to master, but fortunately, as one uses it, the whole matter becomes clearer. It is easier to deal with in this special type of work because an annual in vegetative condition would still be a seedling, probably not having had time to stool out very extensively. A perennial grass in the spring would have some thickened structures present in the crown or culm base, where the food necessary for the initiation of the young growth was stored over the winter. Also, the old culm bases and leaf sheaths of the previous year are more apt to be present on a juvenile perennial grass. Of course, a perennial in its first season's growth might resemble an annual seedling.

2. *Rhizomes.* These are prostrate, more or less elongated stems growing partly or completely below the surface. They bear scales on the young growth or the scars where the scales finally were shed. Sometimes these rhizomes are left in the ground when the culms are pulled up and should always be checked for at the time the grass is collected. The presence of a rhizome would indicate a perennial grass. (Figure 10-1.)

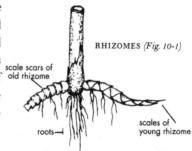

RHIZOMES *(Fig. 10-1)*

scale scars of old rhizome

roots

scales of young rhizome

3. *Stolons.* These are specialized culms that are trailing on the surface of the ground and rooting at the nodes. Like rhizomes, these structures are seldom found on annual grasses. (Figure 10-2.)

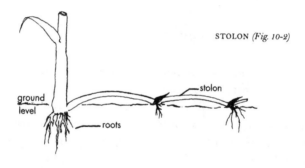

STOLON *(Fig. 10-2)*

stolon

ground level

roots

4. *Sheaths.* Whether or not the sheaths are open or closed for most of their length seems to be the most useful character. Sometimes a closed sheath is torn by the pressure of the expanding inner leaves of the shoot, and this possibility must always be taken into consideration.

The shape of the sheath in cross-section seems to be fairly constant. The relative type of surface (glabrous, scabrous, hairy, etc.) is also a useful character. (Figure 10-3.)

5. *Blades.* The length and width of the leaf blades, as well as the lower and upper surface types, are often very usable characters. Most grass blades have a narrow whitish marginal band which commonly bears a row of little barbs or rough teeth.

The nerves may be raised on either surface. When they are protruded above, the leaf is inclined to roll in from the edges. Blades in cross-section may be flat, U-shaped, V-shaped, or rolled. This rolled character is commonly called "involute" in most books. (Figure 10-4.)

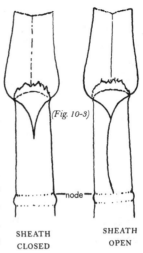

(Fig. 10-3)

node

SHEATH
CLOSED

SHEATH
OPEN

BLADES IN CROSS SECTION *(Fig. 10-4)*

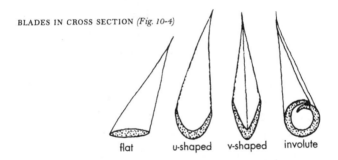

flat   u-shaped   v-shaped   involute

6. *Auricles.* These structures are present on some grasses, especially in the tribe *Hordeae.* In some species they may be absent on some of the leaves or present as rudimentary structures only. (Figure 10-5.)

AURICLES *(Fig. 10-5)*

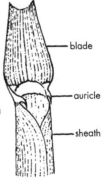

blade

auricle

sheath

7. *Collars.* These are bands or tissue, usually lighter in color than the rest of

93

the leaf, located at the junction of the sheaths and the blades. Extra long hairs are sometimes present on these collars, especially on their front margins. (Figure 10-6.)

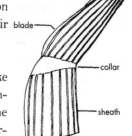

COLLAR *(Fig. 10-6)*

blade

collar

sheath

8. *Ligules.* These collar-like structures furnish the most constant and usable characters of all the vegetative ones. Their shape, margins, and general structure seem remarkably uniform for a species, and even their length seems to vary within certain usable limits. The ligules also furnish surprisingly good generic characters in most grasses. (Figure 10-7.)

9. *Vernation.* This is the way young leaf blades are arranged as they lie inside the outer sheaths of the developing shoot. It seems to be constant for the species, at least throughout a local area. The vernation can be determined by making an external observation of the leaf blade as it unfolds from the sheaths. An even better way is to cut across the sheath at a point just below the collar of the last or uppermost

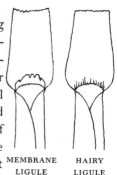

MEMBRANE LIGULE   HAIRY LIGULE

(Fig. 10-7)

fully emerged leaf. Use a sharp blade; the inner leaf blades will not be disturbed and their vernation can be readily ascertained. Each drawing consists of the cross-section of a young shoot.

(1) *Folded (or conduplicate).* The edges meet but do not overlap. (Figure 10-8.)

FOLDED VERNATION (CONDUPLICATE)
(Fig. 10-8)

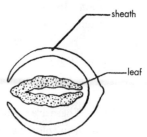

sheath

leaf

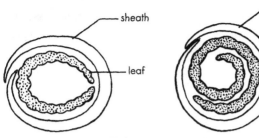

CLASPING VERNATION *(Fig. 10-9)*   ROLLED VERNATION
(CONVOLUTE) *(Fig. 10-10)*

(2) *Clasping.* The edges do not overlap, but the leaf is not so flattened as in "folded." (Figure 10-9.)

(3) *Rolled (convolute).* The edges overlap, one inside the other, like "convolute" in cross-section. (Figure 10-10.)

Folded vernation is usually associated with a sheath that is flattened in cross-section and the folded condition with a round sheath, but there are striking exceptions to the general rule.

10. *Undeveloped inflorescences.*

In "Value of Characters of the Undeveloped Shoot in Identifying Plants," published in *Science* (1939, p. 157–8), I called attention to the fact that a grass shoot can be split and the young incipient inflorescence observed before it emerges. Usually this lies about at ground level and may be rather small in size. The type of inflorescence, often the number of florets to a spikelet, the presence of awns, etc., can usually be made out with a good lens. In some cases these characters will allow for keying down the plant in ordinary grass manuals but their greatest value will probably be in helping decide between two possibilities or in giving confirmation to what would be an otherwise doubtful identification.

These general vegetative characters often help out in identifying grasses in flower or fruiting condition. For example, if *Danthonia* and *Avena* were ever confused by anyone on the basis of spikelet characters, they could readily be separated by differences in the type of ligule—*Avena* having a membranous one, *Danthonia* a hairy one. Of course, this information may not be on record in the manual used, but when it is available, it may be of value in the general identification of grasses.

SOURCES

1. To reiterate, most of the treatments cover the grasses of a local area (such as a state) and deal with a limited number of plants, usually the "common" ones. One must guard against the possibility that the grass checked is not in the publication at all. This is more likely to happen if the plant is rare or only locally common. When the plant is not included at all, there is a tendency to run it down to a similar species that is in the key.

2. List of publications. (Alphabetically arranged by authors. Many are now out of print.)

(1) Ball, Water D. 1927. "Seedling characters of range and pasture grasses." Unpublished thesis. Colorado State College.

(2) Carrier, Lyman. 1917. *The Identification of Grasses by Their Vegetative Characters.* U.S. Dept. Agri. Bul. 461.

(3) Clark, S. E. 1944. *The Identification of Certain Native and Naturalized Grasses by Their Vegetative Characters.* Pub. No. 762; Tech. Bul. 50. Dominion of Canada, Dept. of Agri.

(4) Copple, R. F. and A. E. Aldous. 1932. *The Identification of Certain Native and Naturalized Grasses by Their Vegetative Characters.* Kans. Agri. Exp. Sta. Tech. Bul. 32. Kansas State College of Agriculture.

(5) Copple, R. F. and C. P. Pase. 1967. *A Vegetative Key to Some Common Arizona Range Grasses.* Rocky Mt. Forest and Range Exp. Station Research Paper RM-27.

(6) Harrington. H. D. 1938. *Key to Some Colorado Grasses (Based on Vegetative Characters).* Mimeographed by Author. Colorado State College.

(7) Harrington, H. D. 1944. *Key to Some Colorado Grasses in Vegetative Condition.* Tech. Bul. 33. Colo. Agri. Exp. Station.

(8) Hormay, A. L. 1942. *A Key for Identifying Some Important Annual Range Grasses in Immature Stage.* Calif. Forest and Range Exp. Sta. Res. Note 26.

(9) Hitchcock, C. Leo. *Key to the Grasses of Montana (Based on Vegetative Characters).* Published by author. University of Montana.

(10) Hitchcock, C. Leo., A. Cronquist, and M. Ownbey. 1969. *Vascular Plants of the Pacific Northwest.* Part I. Seattle: Univ. of Wash. Press.

(11) Keim, F. D., G. W. Beadle, and A. L. Frolick. 1932. *The Identification of the More Important Prairie Hay Grasses of Nebraska (By Their Vegetative Characters).* Res. Bul. 65. College of Agriculture, University of Nebraska.

(12) Norton, J. B. S. 1930. *Maryland Grasses.* Bul. 323. University of Maryland.

(13) Nowosad, F. S., D. E. Newton Swales, and W. F. Dore. 1936. *The Identification of Certain Native and Naturalized Hay and Pasture Grasses (By Their Vegetative Characters).* Tech. Bul. 16. Macdonald College, Canada.

(14) Pechanec, Jos. F. 1936. *The Identification of Grasses on the Upper Snake River Plains (By Their Vegetative Characters).* Ecology 17: 479–490.

XI

Illustrated Glossary

A. A prefix meaning "without" as in "apetalous."

Abaxial. Situated on the side or end opposite from the axis. Compare *adaxial.* (Figure 11-1.)

ABAXIAL *(Fig. 11-1)*

Abortive. Imperfectly developed; rudimentary.

Acerose. Needle-shaped, as the leaves of a spruce tree. (Figure 11-2.)

ACEROSE *(Fig. 11-2)*

Achene. A small, dry, rather hard-walled, indehiscent, one-celled, one-seeded fruit, the seed connected to the hull at only one point. (Figure 11-3.)

Acicular. Shaped like a needle, as the "needle" of a pine tree. About the same as *acerose.*

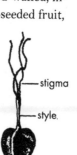

stigma

style.

ACHENE *(Fig. 11-3)*

Acuminate. Tapering to the apex, the sides more or less pinched in before reaching the tip. Compare *acute*. (Figure 11-4.)

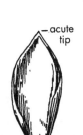

ACUMINATE *(Fig. 11-4)*

Acute. Tapering to the apex with the sides straight or nearly so; usually less tapering than *acuminate*. (Figure 11-5.)

— acute tip

ACUTE *(Fig. 11-5)*

Adaxial. Situated on the side or end next to the axis. Compare *abaxial*. (Figure 11-6.)

ADAXIAL *(Fig. 11-6)*

Adventitious. Developing in an unusual position, usually used for roots. A root that arises from any place other than the *radicle* (primary root system). (Figure 11-7.)

Aerial. In the air, as roots borne above the ground or water.

Aggregate. Crowded into a dense cluster but not united.

Agrostology. The study of grasses (sometimes includes grasslike plants).

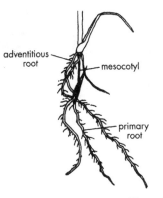

adventitious root

mesocotyl

primary root

ADVENTITIOUS *(Fig. 11-7)*

Alpine. The area above timberline.

Amphibious. Usually growing submerged but may survive for long periods outside of the water.

Androecium. The collective name for the stamens.

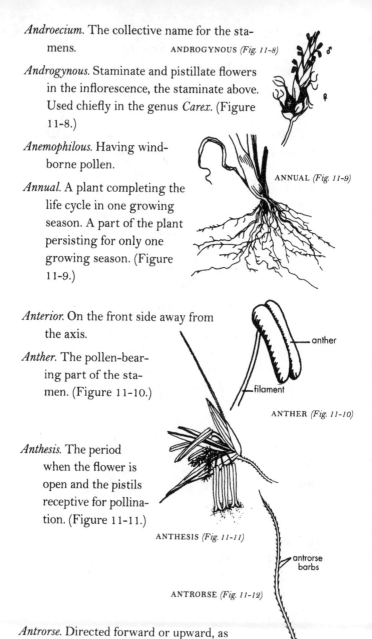

ANDROGYNOUS *(Fig. 11-8)*

Androgynous. Staminate and pistillate flowers in the inflorescence, the staminate above. Used chiefly in the genus *Carex.* (Figure 11-8.)

Anemophilous. Having wind-borne pollen.

ANNUAL *(Fig. 11-9)*

Annual. A plant completing the life cycle in one growing season. A part of the plant persisting for only one growing season. (Figure 11-9.)

Anterior. On the front side away from the axis.

Anther. The pollen-bearing part of the stamen. (Figure 11-10.)

anther

filament

ANTHER *(Fig. 11-10)*

Anthesis. The period when the flower is open and the pistils receptive for pollination. (Figure 11-11.)

ANTHESIS *(Fig. 11-11)*

antrorse barbs

ANTRORSE *(Fig. 11-12)*

Antrorse. Directed forward or upward, as with hairs. (Figure 11-12.)

bristle

Aphyllopodic. Lower leaves bladeless or nearly so; used in sedges. (Figure 11-13.)

APHYLLOPODIC *(Fig. 11-13)*

Apiculate. Ending in an abrupt slender tip which is usually not stiff. (Figure 11-14.)

Appendage. An attached secondary part to main structure.

APICULATE *(Fig. 11-14)*

Appressed. Lying flat or close against something. Often used for hairs. See *retrorse* and *antrorse.*

Approximate. Close together but not united.

Aquatic. Living in water.

ARCUATE *(Fig. 11-15)*

Arcuate. Arched or curving upward like a bow. (Figure 11-15.)

ARISTATE *(Fig. 11-16)*

Aristate. With an awn or stiff bristle, usually at the apex. (Figure 11-16.)

Aristulate. Minutely aristate.

Armed. Provided with thorns, spines, prickles, or sharp hairs.

lemma

Articulation. A joint or node that may pull apart. See *disarticulation.* (Figure 11-17.)

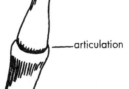

articulation

ARTICULATION *(Fig. 11-17)*

Ascending. Growing obliquely
  upward, often curving upward at about 40° to 60°.
  (Figure 11-18.)

ASCENDING *(Fig. 11-18)*

Asperous. Rough or harsh to the
  touch. See *scabrous.*

Asymmetrical. Without symmetry, the two
  sides unequal.

Attenuate. Gradually narrowing to a tip or
  base, this usually narrow and slender.
  (Figure 11-19.)

attenuate
apex

ATTENUATE *(Fig. 11-19)*

Auricle. Ear-shaped appendages, those
  often occurring in pairs, situated
  at the top of the leaf sheath.
  (Figure 11-20.)

Auriculate. With auricles.

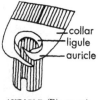

collar
ligule
auricle

AURICLE *(Fig. 11-20)*

Awl-shaped. Tapering gradually upward from a broader base to a
  sharp point, narrowly triangular; usually small structures.
  (Figure 11-21.)

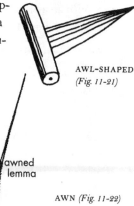

AWL-SHAPED
(Fig. 11-21)

Awn. A more or less stiff
  bristle on the bracts or
  scales, usually a prolon-
  gation of a nerve.
  (Figure 11-22.)

awned
lemma

AWN *(Fig. 11-22)*

Axile. In the axil, the angle between an organ and its axis. See *axillary.*

Axillary. In or related to the axis.

Axis. The elongated central supporting structure, often called a rachis.

BARBED *(Fig. 11-23)*

Barbed. With rigid, short, reflexed processes, like the barbs of a fish-hook. (Figure 11-23.)

barbed bristle

Barbellate. Finely barbed, usually down the sides of the structure as well as at the apex.

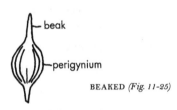

Basifixed. Attached at its base. Compare *versatile.* (Figure 11-24.)

basifixed anther

BASIFIXED *(Fig. 11-24)*

beak

Beaked. With a hard, firm point or projection. (Figure 11-25.)

perigynium

BEAKED *(Fig. 11-25)*

BEARDED *(Fig. 11-26)*

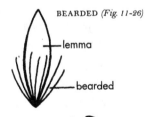

lemma

Bearded. Furnished with long, often stiff hairs. (Figure 11-26.)

bearded

Biconvex. Convex on both sides like a lens. (Figure 11-27.)

BICONVEX *(Fig. 11-27)*

Bidentate. With two teeth, usually at apex. (Figure 11-28.)

Biennial. Living for two years.

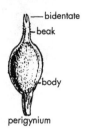

BIDENTATE *(Fig. 11-28)*

perigynium

Bifid. Two-cleft or two-lobed, usually at the apex. (Figure 11-29.)

BIFID *(Fig. 11-29)*

Bifurcate. Divided into two forks or branches. (Figure 11-30.)

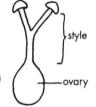

BIFURCATE *(Fig. 11-30)*

BILOBED *(Fig. 11-31)*

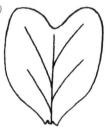

Bilobed. With two lobes, often at the apex. (Figure 11-31.)

Bladder. An inflated, thin-walled structure.

Blade. The expanded, usually flattened portion of a leaf or petal. Compare *sheath.* (Figure 11-32.)

Bloom. A whitish, powdery, glaucous, usually waxy covering of a surface. Also used in reference to a flower.

Body. The main structure or mass of a part, usually of a bract.

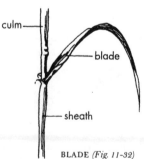

BLADE *(Fig. 11-32)*

Bract. A more or less modified leaf situated near a flower or inflorescence. See *scale, lemma, palea, glume,* and *involucre.*

Bracteate. Having bracts.

Bracteole. Same as bractlet.

Bractlet. A secondary bract as one on the pedicel of a flower, usually smaller than the bracts. Also sometimes used for a very small bract. (Figure 11-33.)

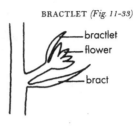

BRACTLET *(Fig. 11-33)*

Branch. A lateral stem, may be a culm or an inflorescence. (See *secondary branch* and *primary branch.*)

Bristle. A stiff, hairlike structure on the order of a pig bristle. (Figure 11-34.)

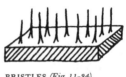

BRISTLES *(Fig. 11-34)*

Bud. The rudimentary state of a stem or branch. Also used for an unexpanded flower.

Bulb. A swollen, thickened structure often made up of fleshly scales. Loosely used for *corm.* (Figure 11-35.)

BULB *(Fig. 11-35)*

longitudinal section

Bulliform cells. Large, thin-walled epidermal cells present on the leaf blades, usually the upper (adaxial) surface.

Bur. A structure, usually containing one or more seeds and bearing spines or prickles, these usually hooked or barbed. (Figure 11-36.)

BUR (CENCHRUS) *(Fig. 11-36)*

Caducous. Falling off unusually early as compared with similar structures in general.

Caespitose. Growing in tufts. Also written *cespitose.* The illustration shows the base of a plant with many caespitose stems. (Figure 11-37.)

CAESPITOSE *(Fig. 11-37)*

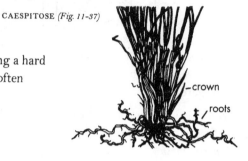

Callous. Having a hard texture, often swollen.

— crown

roots

Callus. A hard protuberance or callosity. In grasses the indurated downward extension of the lemma often morphologically a part of the rachilla. (Figure 11-38.)

CALLUS *(Fig. 11-38)*

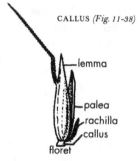

lemma

palea

rachilla

callus

floret

Canaliculate. Longitudinally channeled or grooved. The drawing shows a fruit cut transversely. (Figure 11-39.)

CANALICULATE *(Fig. 11-39)*

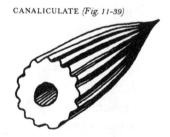

Canescent. With gray or white short hairs, short-hoary. Often loosely used to mean a gray or white surface. (Figure 11-40.)

CANESCENT *(Fig. 11-40)*

Capillary. Very slender and hairlike.

Capitate. In a globular or head-shaped cluster.

Capitellate. Headlike; a diminutive of capitate.

CAPSULE *(Fig. 11-41)*

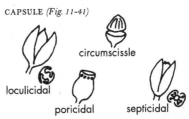

Capsule. A dry, dehiscent fruit made up of more than one carpel. (Figure 11-41.)

circumscissle

loculicidal

poricidal

septicidal

CARINATE *(Fig. 11-42)*

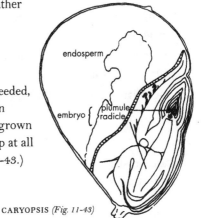

Carinate. Keeled with one or more longitudinal ridges. (Figure 11-42.)

fruit

Cartilaginous. Hard and tough like a cartilage, hence rather elastic.

endosperm

Caryopsis. A dry, one-seeded, indehiscent fruit in which the seed is grown fast to the pericarp at all points. (Figure 11-43.)

embryo { plumule radicle }

CARYOPSIS *(Fig. 11-43)*

Castaneous. Of a chestnut or dark brown color.

Caudate. With a slender, tail-like appendage. (Figure 11-44.)

CAUDATE *(Fig. 11-44)*

Caudex (pl. *caudices*). The persistent, often woody base of an otherwise annual herbaceous stem.

Caulescent. Having a manifest leafy stem above ground. Compare with *acaulescent.* (Figure 11-45.)

CAULESCENT *(Fig. 11-45)*

Cauline. Of or pertaining to the stem.

Cell. A microscopic structural unit of a plant. When used in connection with a pistil, then the same as *locule.*

Cellular. Made up of small pits or compartments.

Centimeter (abbreviation *cm.*) Ten millimeters (about 2.54 cm. to an inch).

Chaff. A thin, dry scale or bract.

Chaffy. Possessing or resembling chaff.

Chartaceous. Texture of stiff writing paper, like parchment.

Ciliate. Beset with a marginal fringe of hairs (cilia). (Figure 11-46.)

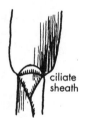

ciliate sheath

Ciliolate. Ciliate but the hairs minute.

CILIATE *(Fig. 11-46)*

CLAVATE *(Fig. 11-47)*

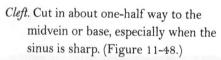

Clavate. Club-shaped and widest nearest the apex. (Figure 11-47.)

Cleft. Cut in about one-half way to the midvein or base, especially when the sinus is sharp. (Figure 11-48.)

Cleistogamous. Flowers that are never exposed for pollination.

CLEFT *(Fig. 11-48)*

Clone. All the individual plants produced asexually from a single plant.

Coleoptile. The sheath of the shoot of the embryo.

Coleorhiza. The sheath of the primary root of the embryo.

Collar. A band of tissue situated at the junction of the blade and sheath. often lighter in color than the rest of the leaf. (See Figure 11-107.)

Collateral. Situated at the side of something.

Column. Used for the parts of various flowers. Also used for the modified bases of the awns in several grass genera (such as Aristida and Andropogon). (Figure 11-49.)

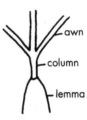

COLUMN *(Fig. 11-49)*

COMA *(Fig. 11-50)*

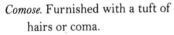

Coma. A tuft of hairs especially at the tips of seeds. (Figure 11-50.)

Comose. Furnished with a tuft of hairs or coma.

Compact. Said of closely packed spikelets or flowers (compare *dense*).

Complete. A flower with sepals, petals, stamens, and pistils present.

Compressed. Flattened, especially laterally.

COMPRESSED-KEELED *(Fig. 11-51)*

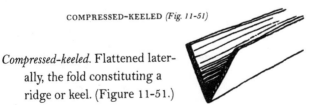

Compressed-keeled. Flattened laterally, the fold constituting a ridge or keel. (Figure 11-51.)

109

Conduplicate. Folded lengthwise down the middle. The leaf in the drawing has been cut transversely. (Figure 11-52.)

CONDUPLICATE *(Fig. 11-52)*

Confluent. Running together; blending in one.

Conical. Cone-shaped, attached at the broad end.

Continuous. Said of a rachis or axis that does not break up at joints at maturity. Compare *articulate.*

Contorted. Twisted or bent or twisted on itself.

CONTRACTED *(Fig. 11-53)*

Contracted. Said of an inflorescence that is narrow and dense with short or appressed branches. (Figure 11-53.)

Convolute. Rolled up longitudinally; technically one edge inside the other but loosely used, especially in grasses. The drawing shows a leaf cut transversely. Commonly called "involute." (Figure 11-54.)

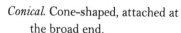

CONVOLUTE *(Fig. 11-54)*

Cordate. Of a conventional heart-shape, the point apical. Compare *obcordate.* (Figure 11-55.)

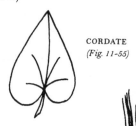

CORDATE *(Fig. 11-55)*

Coriaceous. Leathery in texture.

CORM *(Fig. 11-56)*

Corm. The swollen base of a stem. (Figure 11-56.)

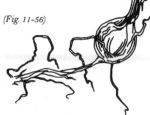

Corrugated. Wrinkled or in folds. (Figure 11-57.)

CORRUGATED *(Fig. 11-57)*

CORYMB *(Fig. 11-58)*

Corymb. A flat-topped or convex open inflorescence; technically a vertically contracted raceme. (Figure 11-58.)

Corymbiform. Shaped like a corymb.

Corymbose. Borne in corymbs or corymblike.

Cotyledon. The embryo leaf in a seed. See *scutellum* and *epiblast.*

Crenate. Toothed with teeth rounded at apex. (Figure 11-59.)

CRENATE *(Fig. 11-59)*

Crenulate. Crenate with small teeth.

Crest. An elevated ridge or projection on the surface.

Crown. The persistent base of a tufted perennial plant, especially a grass. (Figure 11-60.)

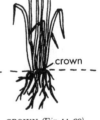

crown

CROWN *(Fig. 11-60)*

Crustose. Of a hard and brittle texture.

Culm. The specialized stem of grasses, sedges and rushes.

Cuneate. Wedge-shaped; rather narrowly triangular, the acute angle downward. (Figure 11-61.)

CUNEATE *(Fig. 11-61)*

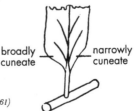

broadly cuneate   narrowly cuneate

Cuspidate. Tipped with an abrupt, short, sharp, firm point. Compare *mucronate.* (Figure 11-62.)

CUSPIDATE *(Fig. 11-62)*

Deciduous. Falling naturally; often said of an awn or a bract. The opposite to *persistent.*

Decumbent. Reclining on the ground but with the end ascending; used for stems. (Figure 11-63.)

DECUMBENT *(Fig. 11-63)*

Decurrent. Extending downward from the point of insertion; said of a leaf decurrent on the stem.

Deflexed. Bent or turned abruptly downward or backward. Same as *reflexed.*

Dehiscent. Opening by definite pores or slits to discharge the contents.

Dense. Said of inflorescences where the flowers (or spikelets) are crowded. Compare *open.*

Dentate. Toothed with the teeth directed outward. Sometimes loosely used for any large teeth. (Figure 11-64.)

DENTATE *(Fig. 11-64)*

Denticles. With minute, usually fragile teeth.

Denticulate. Dentate with small teeth.

Depauperate. Starved or stunted, said of small plants growing under unfavorable conditions.

Depressed. More or less flattened from above.

Dichotomous. Two-forked, the branches equal or nearly so.

Diffuse. Loosely or widely spreading.

Digitate. Compound with the parts radiating out from a common point like the fingers on a hand. Same as *palmate.* (Figure 11-65.)

DIGITATE *(Fig. 11-65)*

Dimorphic. In two forms, usually in the same species.

Dimorphous. With two forms.

Dioecious. Flowers unisexual, the staminate and pistillate borne on separate plants.

Disarticulating. The parts separating at maturity. Compare *articulating.* In the figure the spikelet is disarticulating above the glumes and between the florets. (Figure 11-66.)

DISARTICULATION *(Fig. 11-66)*

Distal. The end opposite the point of attachment.

Distichous. In two vertical ranks, usually conspicuously so. (Figure 11-67.)

Distinct. Separate, or like parts, these not at all united to each other. Compare *connate.*

Divaricate. Widely spreading or diverging.

DISTICHOUS *(Fig. 11-67)*

Dorsal. Referring to the back of a structure. The lower surface of a leaf.

Drooping. Erect to somewhat spreading at base but inclined downward, as the branches of a panicle.

E. A prefix meaning lacking or without, as in *ebracteate.*

Ebracteate. Lacking bracts.

Eccentric. Not situated at the central axis; off-center.

Echinate. Provided with prickles. (Figure 11-68.)

ECHINATE *(Fig. 11-68)*

Ellipsoid. A solid body, elliptic in outline.

Elliptic. Shaped like an ellipse; widest in center and the two ends equal. Loosely used. The drawing shows an average example but the structure can be longer and narrower and still be elliptic. (Figure 11-69.)

ELLIPTIC *(Fig. 11-69)*

Elongate. Narrow, the length many times the width or thickness.

Emarginate. With a shallow notch at the apex. (Figure 11-70.)

EMARGINATE *(Fig. 11-70)* bract

Embryo. The rudimentary plant within a seed. See *caryopsis.*

Endemic. Confined to a limited geographic area.

Endosperm. Substance surrounding the embryo in a seed. See *caryopsis.*

Ensiform. Shaped like a sword. (If a leaf, such as on *Iris.*)

Entire. Margins without teeth or lobes. (Figure 11-71.)

ENTIRE *(Fig. 11-71)*

Epiblast. A small projection often present on the embryo on the side opposite to the *scutellum.* See *caryopsis.*

Epidermis. The outer layer of cells.

Equitant. Leaves that are conduplicate and in two ranks; also two-ranked leaves, flattened with edges toward and away from the axis. (Figure 11-72.)

Erose. Margin irregular as if gnawed.

Erosulate. More or less erose.

Ex. A prefix meaning lacking or without.

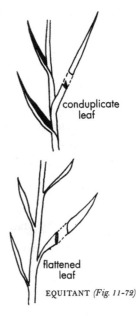

conduplicate leaf

flattened leaf

EQUITANT *(Fig. 11-72)*

Excurrent. Running out or beyond, as a nerve of a bract projecting out beyond the apex. (Figure 11-73.)

nerve

bract

EXCURRENT *(Fig. 11-73)*

Excurved. Curving outward or away from the axis.

Exotic. Not native, introduced from another area. Compare *indigenous.*

Exserted. Projecting beyond a surrounding organ, as a stamen exserted from a bract. Compare *included.*

Extravaginal. A type of branching where the shoot breaks out of the sheath and grows more or less at right angles to it. Compare *intravaginal.* (Figure 11-74.)

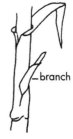

branch

EXTRAVAGINAL *(Fig. 11-74)*

Falcate. An asymmetric shape, flat and curved to one side, tapering upward. (Figure 11-75.)

FALCATE *(Fig. 11-75)*

Fan-shaped. Shaped like an opened folding fan; triangular with the upper side convex. (Figure 11-76.)

FAN-SHAPED *(Fig. 11-76)*

lemma

Farinose. Covering with a mealy, usually whitish substance.

Fascicled. Borne in close bundles or clusters.

Fastigiate. Erect or near together with a broomlike effect.

Ferruginous. Rust-colored.

Fertile. Capable of producing fruit and seeds; flower may be pistillate or perfect.

Fibrillose. With fine fibers. Sometimes written *fibrillate.*

Fibrous. Composed of, or resembling fibers.

FILAMENT *(Fig. 11-77)*

Filament. Any threadlike body; used especially for that part of the stamen that supports the anther. (Figure 11-77.)

anther

filament

Filamentose. Composed of threads. Also written *filamentous.*

Filiferous. Producing or bearing threadlike growths.

Filiform. Threadlike; long, slender, and terete.

Fimbrilla (pl. *fimbrillae*). A single unit of a marginal fringe.

Fistulose. Hollow and cylindrical, often rather enlarged. Also written *fistulous.* (Figure 11-78.)

FISTULOSE *(Fig. 11-78)*

Flabellate. Same as *fan-shaped.*

Flabelliform. Same as *fan-shaped.*

Flaccid. Lax and weak; without rigidity.

Flange. A projecting edge or rim; edge flaring and conspicuous. (Figure 11-79.)

FLANGE *(Fig. 11-79)*

Flexuose. Same as *flexuous.*

FLEXUOUS *(Fig. 11-80)*

Flexuous. Bent alternately in opposite directions, usually not strongly so. (Figure 11-80.)

Floret. A special term for a grass flower with its lemma and palea included. (Figure 11-81.)

lemma

palea

rachilla

FLORET *(Fig. 11-81)*

Flower. A reproductive structure consisting of ovary or stamens (or both), and often also closely enveloping parts.

FLUTED *(Fig. 11-82)*

Fluted. With grooves or furrows. (Figure 11-82.)

Foliaceous. Leaflike, especially in color.

Fruit. The ripened ovary. Also used for any part enclosing as it falls.

Fugacious. Falling or fading very early. About the same as *caducous.*

Fuscous. Dark gray-brown in color.

Fusiform. Spindle-shaped.

Geniculate. Bent abruptly like a
   knee or stovepipe bend.
   Often said of an awn or a
   culm. (Figure 11-83.)

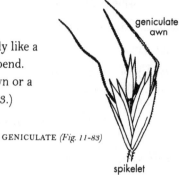

GENICULATE *(Fig. 11-83)*

spikelet

Gibbous. Enlarged, humped, or
   swollen on one side. (Figure
   11-84.)

Glabrate. Becoming glabrous in
   age.

Glabrescent. About the same as
   glabrate.

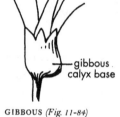

GIBBOUS *(Fig. 11-84)*

gibbous
calyx base

Glabrous. No hairs present at all; also used for smooth.

Gland. A secreting surface or structure or an appendage
   having the general appearance of such an organ.

Glandular. Bearing glands. A glandular hair has enlargement like a hat pin at the apex. (Figure 11-85.)

GLANDULAR HAIRS *(Fig. 11-85)*

Glaucous. Covered with a whitish or bluish waxy covering.
   This covering should rub off readily, but the term is
   sometimes loosely used for any whitish surface, especially in grasses or grasslike plants.

Glaucescent. Tending to be glaucous.

Globose. Shaped like a globe. (Figure 11-86.)

Glomerate. Crowded, congested, or compactly clustered.

GLOBOSE *(Fig. 11-86)*

Glomerule. A dense, crowded cluster of structures.

Glume. A chafflike bract; used particularly for the two lower empty bracts of a grass spikelet. (Figure 11-87.)

Glume, First. The glume inserted slightly lower and just below the first floret. It is usually the smaller of the two or may be absent entirely.

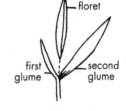
GLUME *(Fig. 11-87)*

Glume, Second. The glume inserted opposite to the first, usually larger. When the first is lacking, the second glume is on the opposite side of the first floret.

Grain. A swollen, seedlike structure; also used as a synonym for *caryopsis.*

Grasslike. Resembling grasses in general appearance, usually used for sedges and rushes.

Gregarious. Tending to grow in clusters or groups.

Gynaecandrous. With staminate and pistillate flowers on the same spike, the pistillate above; used in the genus *Carex.* (Figure 11-88.)

Head. A dense cluster of sessile or nearly sessile structures. These usually floral.

GYNAECANDROUS *(Fig. 11-88)*

Herb. A plant with no persistent woody stem above ground; also plants used in seasoning and medicine.

Herbaceous. Having the characteristic of an herb; also leaflike in color or texture.

Herbarium. A collection of dried pressed plant specimens; also the room or building housing this collection.

Hermaphroditic. A flower with both stamens and pistils. Same as *perfect* and *bisexual.*

Heteromorphous. Of more than one kind or form.

Hilum. The scar where the seed was attached to the ovary wall. In grasses, sometimes loosely used for the scar where the ovary was attached.

Hirsute. With moderately coarse and stiff hairs. (Figure 11-89.)

Hirsutulose. Same as hirsutulous.

Hirsutulous. Somewhat hirsute.

Hirtellous. Minutely hirsute.

HIRSUTE *(Fig. 11-89)*

Hispid. With stiff and rigid bristles or bristlelike hairs, these usually stiff enough to penetrate the skin. (Figure 11-90.)

Hispidulous. Minutely hispid.

Hoary. Covered with white or gray, short, fine hairs.

HISPID *(Fig. 11-90)*

Homomorphous. Of only one form or kind.

Hooked. Abruptly curved at tip. (Figure 11-91.)

HOOKED *(Fig. 11-91)*

Horn. A stiff, tapering appendage somewhat like the horn of a cow. (Figure 11-92.)

Hyaline. Thin in texture, translucent, or transparent. (See *scarious.*)

HORN *(Fig. 11-92)*

Hydrophyte. A plant that grows in water. Compare *mesophyte* and *xerophyte.*

Hygroscopic. Altering form or position due to changes in moisture content.

Imbricate. Partly overlapping like shingles on a roof, either vertically, laterally, or both. (Figure 11-93.)

Immersed. Growing submerged in water.

Imperfect flowers. Lacking either stamens or pistils. Compare *perfect, unisexual,* and *bisexual.*

Implicate. Tangled, as the branches of some panicles.

IMBRICATE *(Fig. 11-93)*

Included. Not at all protruding from the surrounding organ. Compare *exserted.*

Incurved. Curved toward the axis or attachment.

Indehiscent. Remaining persistently closed; not opening by definite lines or pores.

Indigenous. Native to the area. Compare *exotic.*

Indurated. Hardened and stiffened, often with a shiny surface.

Inflated. Bladderlike; enlarged with thin walls.

Inflexed. Turned abruptly or bent inwards; incurved.

Inflorescence. The flowering part of a plant, almost always used for a flower cluster. In grasses, the spikelets and the branches or axis bearing them.

Innovation. A basal offshoot from the main stem, shorter and less modified than a rhizome or stolon; in grasses, an incomplete young shoot. (Figure 11-94.)

primary plant

innovation

INNOVATION *(Fig. 11-94)*

Intercostal. The area between the veins or nerves.

Internerves. The spaces between the nerves or veins.

Internode. The portion of a stem or other structure between two nodes. (Figure 11-95.)

Interrupted. The order or continuity broken as an inflorescence with gaps in the order.

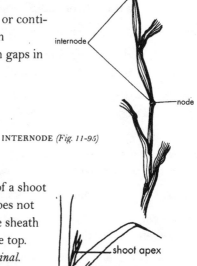

INTERNODE *(Fig. 11-95)*

Intravaginal. Growth of a shoot where the apex does not break through the sheath but emerges at the top. Compare *extravaginal*. (Figure 11-96.)

INTRAVAGINAL *(Fig. 11-96)*

Introduced. A plant brought in intentionally from another area, as for purposes of cultivation. Such a plant may later escape and persist.

Involucel. A secondary *involucre*.

Involucrate. With an *involucre*.

Involucre. A more or less distinct whorl of reduced leaves, branchlets, or bracts subtending a flower or inflorescence. (Figure 11-97.)

INVOLUCRE *(Fig. 11-97)*

Involute. Both edges inrolled toward the midnerve on the upper surface; loosely used in grasses for any leaf rolled on the upper surface. Compare *revolute*. (Figure 11-98.)

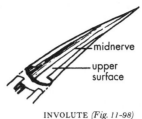

INVOLUTE *(Fig. 11-98)*

Joint. The node of a grass stem. The internode of a rachis that is articulated; also used for an articulation itself.

Keel. A dorsal, projecting, usually central rib, like the keel of a boat. (Figure 11-99.)

Lacerate. Margins irregularly cut or cleft, as if torn.

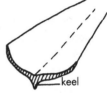

KEEL *(Fig. 11-99)*

Laciniate. Narrowly incised or slashed; margins cut in narrow and usually pointed lobes. (Figure 11-100.)

LACINIATE *(Fig. 11-100)*

Lacuna. An air space in the midst of tissue.

Lamina. The blade of a leaf as distinguished from the *sheath*. See *blade*.

Lanate. With long, tangled, woolly hairs. (Figure 11-101.)

LANATE *(Fig. 11-101)*

LANCEOLATE *(Fig. 11-102)*

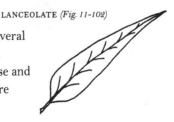

Lanceolate. Lance-shaped; several times longer than wide, broadest toward the base and tapering to apex. (Figure 11-102.)

Lateral. Borne on the sides of a structure or object.

Laterally compressed. Flattened from the sides as spikelets, florets, glumes, and lemmas. Compare *dorsally flattened.* (Figure 11-103.)

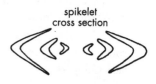

spikelet cross section

LATERALLY COMPRESSED *(Fig. 11-103)*

Lax. Loose; often used for a soft open inflorescence or for soft drooping stems or foliage.

Leaf. The lateral organ of a stem usually consisting of a sheath and a blade. (Figure 11-104.)

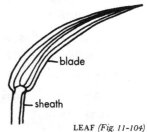

blade

sheath

LEAF *(Fig. 11-104)*

Lemma. The lower of the two bracts enclosing a grass flower above the glumes; formerly called "flowering glume." (Figure 11-105.)

LEMMA *(Fig. 11-105)*

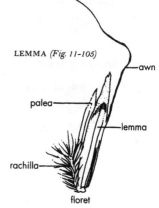

awn

palea

lemma

rachilla

floret

LENS-SHAPED *(Fig. 11-106)*

Lens-shaped. Shaped like a typical lens, rather flattened with the both sides convex. (Figure 11-106.)

Lenticular. Lens-shaped; *biconvex* in shape. (See *biconvex* for drawing.)

Ligulate. Furnished with a *ligule.*

Ligule. A hairlike or membranous projection up from the inside of a grass sheath at its junction with the blade. (Figure 11-107.)

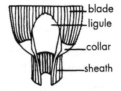

LIGULE *(Fig. 11-107)*

Linear. Narrow and flat with sides parallel, like a typical grass leaf blade. (Figure 11-108.)

Lobe. Any segment of an organ, especially if rounded. See *lobed.*

LINEAR *(Fig. 11-108)*

Lobed. Bearing lobes; loosely used but technically cut in not more than halfway to the base or midvein, the sinuses and apex of segments rounded. (Figure 11-109.)

LOBED *(Fig. 11-109)*

Locule. The cell or compartment of an ovary, fruit, or anther.

Lodicule. Small scales or bumps, usually two in number and situated near the edges of the lemma. They are thought to be vestiges of the flower *perianth.* (Figure 11-110.)

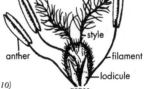

LODICULE *(Fig. 11-110)*

Loose. Open, often said of a *panicle.* Compare *dense* or *compact.* (Figure 11-111.)

LOOSE *(Fig. 11-111)*

Macrohair. Thick-walled hairs of the leaf epidermis.

Many. Eleven or more. Same as *numerous.*

Mealy. A surface covered with minute particles, these usually rounded.

Medial. Refers to the middle of a structure.

Membranaceous. Same as *membranous.*

Membranous. Thin, soft, like a membrane, often more or less transparent. However, in our plants, used for a fairly thin, run-of-the-mill texture usually more or less green in color.

Meristem. Any tissue with undifferentiated cells capable of cell division.

Mesophyll. The photosynthetic tissue of a leaf lying between the opposing epidermal layers.

Mesophyte. A plant that grows under medium or average conditions, especially of moisture supply. Compare *hydrophyte* and *xerophyte.*

Meter (abbreviation *M.* or *m.*). Unit of measurement consisting of 100 centimeters; almost 40 inches.

Microhair. Small, often thin-walled epidermal hairs. Compare *macrohair.*

Micron. A microscopic unit of measurement, 1/1000 of a millimeter.

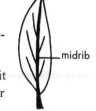

MIDRIB *(Fig. 11-112)*

Midrib. The main or central rib of a structure. (Figure 11-112.)

Millimeter (abbreviation *mm.*). A small unit of measurement, 1/10 of a centimeter or about 1/25 of an inch.

Monoecious. Flowers unisexual, but the staminate and pistillate ones borne on the same plant. An outstanding example would be found in corn (*Zea*). (Figure 11-113.)

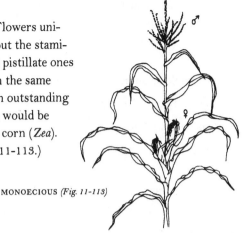

MONOECIOUS *(Fig. 11-113)*

Monotypic. When referring to a genus, then one with only a single species in it.

Mucro. A short, small, abrupt, toothlike tip, but not very sharp at extreme apex. Compare *cuspidate.* (Figure 11-114.)

Mucronate. Tipped with a *mucro.*

Mucronulate. Minutely mucronate, the mucro very small.

MUCRO *(Fig. 11-114)*

Multicipital. With many heads, referring to the crown of a single root or to several caudices.

Muricate. Roughened with short, hard points. (Figure 11-115.)

Muriculate. Very finely *muricate.*

Muticous. Blunt and without a point.

MURICATE *(Fig. 11-115)*

Naked. Lacking some structure, appendage, or hairs which might ordinarily be expected to be present.

NAVICULAR *(Fig. 11-116)*

Navicular. Boat-shaped, applied particularly to the boat-shaped tip of leaf blades. (Figure 11-116.)

Needlelike. Long, slender, rather rigid, more or less sharp at apex like a needle. Usually rounded or square in cross-section but sometimes flattened. See *acerose* for drawing.

Nerve. A simple or unbranched vein or slender rib.

Nerviform. On the order of a nerve.

Netted. Same as reticulated.

Net-veined. The veins joining together on the order of a fish net.

Neuter. Without functional stamens or pistils. Same as *neutral.*

Neutral. See *neuter.*

Nodding. Inclined more or less from a stiff, upright position, as a panicle. (Figure 11-117.)

NODDING *(Fig. 11-117)*

Node. The place on a stem where leaves or branches normally originate; the place on an axis that bears other structures; any swollen or knob-like structure. See *internode* for a figure.

Nodose. Knobby or knotty.

Nodulose. Provided with minute knobs.

Numerous. Eleven or more. Same as *many.*

Ob. A prefix signifying inversion; see *obconical.*

Obcompressed. Flattened opposite to the usual way, e.g., flattened dorso-ventrally instead of laterally.

Obconical. Inversely cone-shaped, attached at the pointed end. (Figure 11-118.)

OBCONICAL *(Fig. 11-118)*

Obcordate. Inverted heart-shape, attached at the point. Also used in reference to a deeply notched apex irrespective of the general shape. (Figure 11-119.)

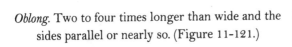

OBCORDATE *(Fig. 11-119)*

Oblanceolate. Inversely lanceolate; attached at the tapered end. (Figure 11-120.)

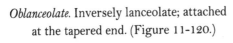

OBLANCEOLATE *(Fig. 11-120)*

Oblong. Two to four times longer than wide and the sides parallel or nearly so. (Figure 11-121.)

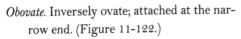

OBLONG *(Fig. 11-121)*

Obovate. Inversely ovate; attached at the narrow end. (Figure 11-122.)

Obovoid. A three-dimensional figure of *obovate* outline.

Obsolete. Rudimentary or not at all evident; applied particularly to organs usually present.

OBOVATE *(Fig. 11-122)*

Obtuse. Blunt or rounded at the apex. (Figure 11-123.)

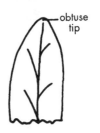

obtuse tip

OBTUSE *(Fig. 11-123)*

Open. Loose, not compact or dense. Said especially of a *panicle* with spreading branches. (Figure 11-124.)

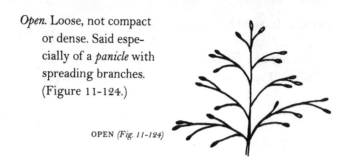

OPEN *(Fig. 11-124)*

Opposite. Structures two at a node and situated across from each other.

Orbicular. A two-dimensional figure circular in outline. Compare *spherical.* (Figure 11-125.)

ORBICULAR *(Fig. 11-125)*

Oval. Loosely used for broadly elliptical, the width over one-half the length. Some authors have used it interchangeably with *ovate.* (Figure 11-126.)

OVAL *(Fig. 11-126)*

OVARY *(Fig. 11-127)*

Ovary. That part of the pistil that contains the *ovule* or ovules. (Figure 11-127.)

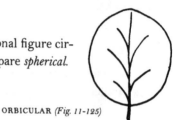

Ovate. Egg-shaped in outline; attached at the wide end. (Figure 11-128.)

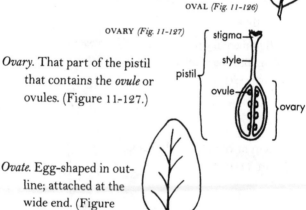

OVATE *(Fig. 11-128)*

Ovoid. A three-dimensional figure, ovate in outline.

Ovule. The structure that develops into the seed. See *ovary* for drawing.

Palea (pl. *paleae* or *paleas*). The inner of the two bracts, enclosed by the edges of the *lemma*. See *lemma* for drawing.

Paleaceous. Chaffy, thin, small, and often rather translucent.

Palustrine. Inhabiting wet ground; marsh-dwelling.

Pandurate. Fiddle-shaped. Same as *panduriform.* (Figure 11-129.)

PANDURATE *(Fig. 11-129)*

Panduriform. Same as *pandurate.*

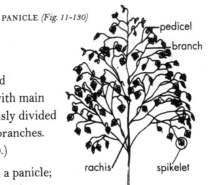

PANICLE *(Fig. 11-130)*

—pedicel

—branch

Panicle. A compound inflorescence with main axis and variously divided or subdivided branches. (Figure 11-130.)

Paniculate. Borne in a panicle; resembling a panicle.

rachis

spikelet

Papery. Thin and usually whitish like paper. Compare with *chartaceous.*

Papilla (pl. *papillae*). A minute, nipple-shaped projection. (Figure 11-131.)

PAPILLA *(Fig. 11-131)*

Papillose. Bearing *papillae.*

Parallel veined. A structure with veins running parallel to each other, usually all about the same size (except sometimes at midrib) and the connections between obscure. Characteristic of the leaf of *Monocotyledoneae.* (Figure 11-132.)

PARALLEL VEINED *(Fig. 11-132)*

Parted. Lobed or cut in over halfway and usually very near to the base or midrib. The sinuses and segments may be sharp or rounded. (Figure 11-133.)

PARTED *(Fig. 11-133)*

Pectinate. Pinnatifid with the segments narrow and arranged like the teeth of a comb; comblike. (Figure 11-134.)

PECTINATE *(Fig. 11-134)*

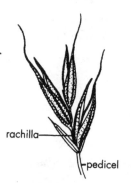

Pedicel. The stalk to a single flower of an inflorescence; also used as a stalk to a grass spikelet. Compare *peduncle.* (Figure 11-135.)

Pedicellate. Borne on a *pedicel.*

Pedicelled. With a pedicel. Same as *pedicellate.*

rachilla

pedicel

PEDICEL *(Fig. 11-135)*

Penduncle. The stalk to a solitary flower (or unit) or to an inflorescence. Compare *pedicel.*

Pendunculate. Borne upon a *peduncle.*

Pendant. Same as *pendulous.*

Pendulous. More or less hanging or declined.

Perennial. A plant lasting for three or more years; a stem not dying back over winter.

Perfect. A flower with both functional stamens and pistils.

Perianth. The floral envelope consisting of calyx and corolla; however, incomplete or modified. Used particularly when the calyx and corolla cannot be readily distinguished.

Pericarp. The ripened outer wall of the matured fruit.

Perigynium. The bract in the pistillate flower of sedges that completely surrounds the pistil. It is often inflated and usually almost or completely joined at the edges. (Figure 11-136.)

PERIGYNIUM *(Fig. 11-136)*

Persistent. Remaining attached after similar structures are apt to fall. Also used as the opposite to *deciduous.*

Petal. One of the individual parts of the corolla, used particularly for a polypetalous corolla in designating one unit.

Petiole. The stalk to a leaf blade or to a compound leaf. (Figure 11-137.)

PETIOLE *(Fig. 11-137)*

Pilose. With long, soft, straight hairs. In our group of plants, this is used about the same as *villous.* (Figure 11-138.)

PILOSE *(Fig. 11-138)*

133

Pistil. The seed-producing organ consisting usually of ovary, style, and stigma. (Figure 11-139.)

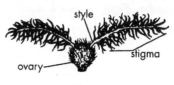

PISTIL *(Fig. 11-139)*

Pistillate. Provided with pistils, used when stamens are lacking.

Pith. The spongy center of a stem.

Pitted. Marked with small depressions or pits. (Figure 11-140.)

PITTED *(Fig. 11-140)*

Phyllopodic. Lower leaves of the culms with well-developed blades. Used in sedges. Compare *aphyllopodic*.

Plane. With flat surface.

Plano-convex. An object—usually a fruit or seed—flat on one side and convex on the other. The drawing shows a seed cut in two sections. (Figure 11-141.)

PLANO-CONVEX *(Fig. 11-141)*

Plicate. Folded in plaits, usually lengthwise on the order of a folding fan. (Figure 11-142.)

PLICATE *(Fig. 11-142)*

Plumbeous. The color of lead, greenish-drab.

Plumose. Hairs with side hairs along the main axis like the plume of a feather. (Figure 11-143.)

Plumule. The stem- and leaf-producing structure of an embryo in the seed. See *caryopsis* for drawing.

PLUMOSE *(Fig. 11-143)*

Pollen. The male spores in an anther.

Polymorphous. With several forms; variable as to habit.

Posterior. On the side next to or close to the axis. Compare *anterior*.

Prickle. A small, usually slender out-growth of the young bark, coming off with it. Compare *spine* and *thorn*. (Figure 11-144.)

PRICKLE *(Fig. 11-144)*

Procumbent. Lying or trailing on the ground, usually not rooting at the nodes. See *prostrate*. (Figure 11-145.)

PROCUMBENT *(Fig. 11-145)*

Proliferous. Producing bulbs or plantlets from leaves or other offshoots.

Prophyllum (prophyll). The first leaf of a lateral shoot.

Prostrate. Lying flat on the ground; if a stem, then may or may not root at nodes. See *procumbent* for drawing.

Proximad. Toward the point of attachment.

Proximal. The end of an organ by which it is attached.

Pruinose. With waxy, powdery, usually whitish covering, this often rubbing off readily; *glaucous* to a conspicuous degree.

Pseudo-. A prefix meaning false.

Puberulent. With very short hairs; minutely *pubescent*. (Figure 11-146.)

PUBERULENT *(Fig. 11-146)*

Pubescent. Loosely used to signify covered with hairs; technically, with soft, short hairs. (Figure 11-147.)

PUBESCENT *(Fig. 11-147)*

Pulvinate. Cushioned or shaped like a close, thick mat or cushion.

Pulvinus. A swollen motor organ that causes movement. (Figure 11-148.)

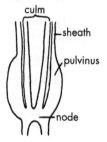

Punctate. Dotted with depressions, or with translucent internal glands or colored dots.

PULVINUS *(Fig. 11-148)*

Puncticulate. Minutely *punctate.*

Pungent. Tipped with a sharp, rigid point.

Pustulose. Beset with pimple-like or blister-like elevated areas. Same as *pustulate.*

Pyramidal. Shaped like a pyramid. Often applied to cone-shaped *panicles.*

Pyriform. Pear-shaped. (Figure 11-149.)

PYRIFORM *(Fig. 11-149)*

Raceme. An inflorescence with *pedicelled* units borne along a more or less elongated axis. Uncommon in our plants except to designate a portion of a *panicle.* (Figure 11-150.)

Racemiform. In the form of a *raceme.*

Racemose. Raceme-like or bearing *racemes.*

RACEME *(Fig. 11-150)*

Rachilla. A small rachis; applied particularly to the axis of a grass spikelet, and to the secondary axis in sedges. (Figure 11-151.)

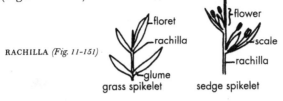

RACHILLA *(Fig. 11-151)*

grass spikelet — floret, rachilla, glume

sedge spikelet — flower, scale, rachilla

Rachis. The central elongated axis to any structure in the inflorescence; often called "main axis." (Figure 11-152.)

RACHIS *(Fig. 11-152)* — spikelet, rachis

Radical. Belonging to the root, or apparently arising from or very near the root.

Rank. A vertical row, for example, leaves that are two-ranked are in two rows along the stem.

Ray. The more or less elongated branch or peduncle of an inflorescence, often used for sedges. (Figure 11-153.)

Reclinate. Turned or bent abruptly downward.

RAY *(Fig. 11-153)* — spike, ray, involucre bract

Reclining. Lying upon something.

Recumbent. Leaning or reposing upon the ground.

Recurved. Curved outward, downward, or backward.

Reduced floret. A staminate or neuter one. Compare *rudimentary.*

Reflexed. Abruptly bent or turned downward or backward.

Regular. A flower with all the members of each set alike in form, size, and color, radially symmetrical.

Reniform. Kidney-shaped. (Figure 11-154.)

Repand. With a wavy surface or margin, not as deep as *sinuate*. Same as *undulate*.

RENIFORM *(Fig. 11-154)*

Reticulate. In the form of a network; leaf veins in a network. (Figure 11-155.)

RETICULATE *(Fig. 11-155)*

Retrorse. Directed backward or downward. (Figure 11-156.)

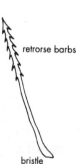

retrorse barbs

bristle

RETRORSE *(Fig. 11-156)*

Retuse. A rounded apex with a shallow notch. (Figure 11-157.)

RETUSE *(Fig. 11-157)*

Revolute. Rolled backward from each margin upon the lower side. Opposite of *involute*. (Figure 11-158.)

REVOLUTE *(Fig. 11-158)*

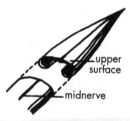

upper surface

midnerve

Rhizomatous. Having the characters of a *rhizome*. Sometimes written *rhizomatose*.

Rhizome. Any prostrate, more or less elongated stem growing partly or completely beneath the surface of the ground; usually rooting at the nodes and becoming upcurved at apex. See *rootstock.* (Figure 11-159.)

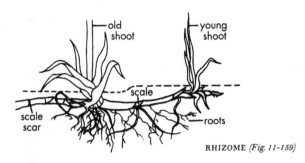

RHIZOME *(Fig. 11-159)*

Rib. A primary or prominent vein of a structure.

Root. The descending axis of the plant, without nodes and internodes and absorbing moisture from the ground. Roots may appear, however, in unusual places. See *adventitious.*

Rootlet. A small root.

Rootstock. A rootlike stem or branch under or sometimes on the ground. Like rhizome but loosely used by some to include any elongated underground structure that spreads the plant.

Rosette. A dense basal cluster of leaves arranged in circular fashion like the leaves of the common dandelion. (Figure 11-160.)

ROSETTE *(Fig. 11-160)*

Rostrate. Having a beak. See *beaked.*

Rosulate. In the form of a *rosette.*

Rudiment. An imperfectly developed, usually minute organ.

Rufous. Reddish-brown in color.

Rugose. With wrinkles or creased surface.

Rugulose. Minutely *rugose*. *Cross-regulose* is laterally wrinkled.

Runner. A very slender or
    filiform *stolon*. (Figure
    11-162.)

RUNNER *(Fig. 11-161)*

Rushlike. Grasslike in general appearance,
    the flowers not brightly-colored or
    conspicuous. (Figure 11-162.)

RUSH–LIKE *(Fig. 11-162)*

Saccate. Sac-shaped or pouch-shaped.

Scaberulent. Slightly *scabrous*.

Scaberulous. Slightly *scabrous*.

Scabrous. Rough or harsh to the touch, usually from very
    short stiff hairs or short, sharp projections. The test is
    to draw the finger tip lightly over the surface. The
    drawing shows a surface
    scabrous from short sharp pro-
    jections. (Figure 11-163.)

SCABROUS *(Fig. 11-163)*

Scale. Any thin, *scarious* body resembling
    the scale of a fish or reptile; often
    used for such structures present on
    the basal or underground portion of
    a plant. Compare *bract*. *Scale* is used
    particularly for the bract subtending
    the sedge flower. (Figure 11-164.)

scale — bract

Scape. A naked flowering stem rising
    from the ground without proper
    leaves.

SCALE *(Fig. 11-164)*

Scapose. Bearing a scape or resembling one.

Scarious. Thin, dry, membranous, and more or less translucent, not green.

Scurfy. Covered with small scale-like or bran-like particles.

Scutellem. A band of tissue situated between the embryonic shoot and the *endosperm.* It acts as an absorbing organ and is considered by many to be a *cotyledon.* (Figure 11-165.)

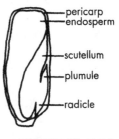

SCUTELLUM *(Fig. 11-165)*

Secondary. Below or less than primary. For example, branches in a panicle rising from the primary ones. (Figure 11-166.)

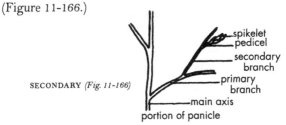

SECONDARY *(Fig. 11-166)*

Secund. Borne or directed to one side of the axis. (Figure 11-167.)

Seed. The matured ovule, consisting of embryo and its coats, with a supply of food. Loosely used in grasses and sedges for a one-seeded fruit.

secund spikelets

SECUND *(Fig. 11-167)*

Seedling. A very young plant, as one growing from a seed.

Self-pollinated. In our group of plants, often used for pollination while the flower is still unopened. See *cleistogamous.*

Sepal. One of the parts of the outer whorl of the floral envelope or calyx, often green in color.

Septate. Divided by one or more partitions.

Septate-nodulose. The large longitudinal veins or nerves bearing lateral veins connecting them at intervals. This makes a kind of net. (Figure 11-168.)

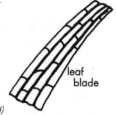

SEPTATE-NODULOSE *(Fig. 11-168)*

Septum. Any kind of partition.

Sericeous. Covered with long, straight, soft, appressed hairs giving a silky texture. The hairs are usually more numerous than in the drawing. (Figure 11-169.)

SERICEOUS *(Fig. 11-169)*

Serrate. With sharp teeth directed forward. Sometimes incorrectly used for any small teeth. (Figure 11-170.)

SERRATE *(Fig. 11-170)*

Serrulate. Serrate with small teeth. See *serrate* for drawing.

Sessile. Without a stalk of any kind. (Figure 11-171.)

SESSILE *(Fig. 11-171)*

Seta (pl. *setae*). A bristle-like hair.

Setaceous. Bristle-like.

Setiform. Like or on the order of a bristle.

Setose. Beset with bristles. (Figure 11-172.)

SETOSE *(Fig. 11-172)*

Sheath. A tubular envelope, usually used for that part of the leaf of a sedge or grass that envelopes the stem. (Figure 11-173.)

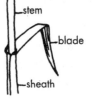

SHEATH *(Fig. 11-173)*

Shrub. A woody perennial plant smaller than a tree and usually with several stems. Compare *tree* with its drawing.

Sigmoid. Double-curved like the letter S. (Figure 11-174.)

SIGMOID *(Fig. 11-174)*

Silky. Of silk-like appearance caused by long, straight, soft, appressed hairs. See *sericeous.*

SINUATE *(Fig. 11-175)*

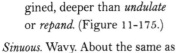

Sinuate. Strongly wavy-margined, deeper than *undulate* or *repand.* (Figure 11-175.)

Sinuous. Wavy. About the same as *sinuate.*

Sinus. The depression or recess between two adjoining lobes. (Figure 11-176.)

Smooth. Surface not rough, sometimes loosely used for absence of any hair.

SINUS *(Fig. 11-176)*

Spathe. A large bract sheathing or enclosing an inflorescence.

Spherical. A three-dimensional solid round in outline, like the shape of the earth. Same as *globose.*

Spicate. Arranged in or resembling a *spike.*

Spicule. Short, stiff-pointed projection on a surface.

Spike. An inflorescence with the flowers *sessile* on a more or less elongated axis. (Figure 11-177.)

Spikelet. A small or secondary *spike,* used particularly in grasses and sedges. In grasses it is a special unit subtended by two glumes (those rarely absent), and containing one or more florets. (Figure 11-178.)

Spikelike. Resembling a spike, used when the flowers or *spikelets* are on short *pedicels* or on very short panicle branches.

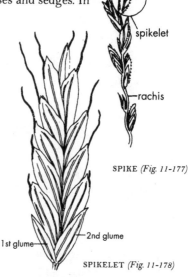

spikelet

rachis

SPIKE *(Fig. 11-177)*

1st glume

2nd glume

SPIKELET *(Fig. 11-178)*

Spine. A sharp-pointed, rigid, deep-seated outgrowth from the stem, not pulling off with the bark. Compare *prickle.* Sometimes differentiated from *thorn* by absence of vascular tissue.

Spinescent. Bearing a spine or ending in a spine-like sharp point.

Spinulose. Minutely spiny; beset with small *spines.*

Sprawling. Lying on or leaning upon or over another object.

Spreading. Diverging nearly at right angles; nearly prostrate.

Squamella (pl. *squamellae*). A small chaffy bract or scale-like appendage.

Squarrose. Having the parts or processes (usually the tips) spreading or *recurved.* (Figure 11-179.)

SQUARROSE *(Fig. 11-179)*

lower units
squarrose

Stamen. One of the pollen-bearing organs of a flower. Made up of *filament* and *anther.* (Figure 11-180.)

—anther

STAMEN *(Fig. 11-180)*

—filament

Staminate. Bearing *stamens* only.

Sterile. Infertile and unproductive, as a flower without a pistil, a stamen without an anther or a leafy shoot without flowers.

Stigma. That part of the pistil that receives the pollen, usually at or near the apex of the pistil and mostly hairy, *papillose,* or sticky. See *ovary* for drawing.

Stigmatic. Belonging to or having the characteristics of a *stigma.*

Stipe. The stalklike support of a structure; if a pistil, then above the other flower parts. (Figure 11-181.)

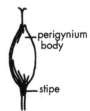

perigynium
body

stipe

STIPE *(Fig. 11-181)*

Stipitate. Provided with a stipe or with a slender stalklike base.

Stolon. A trailing shoot above ground, rooting at the nodes. (Figure 11-182.)

STOLON *(Fig. 11-182)*

Stoloniferous. Bearing *stolons.*

Stoloniform. On the general order of a *stolon.*

Stomate (pl. *stomata*). A small opening on the surface of a leaf through which gaseous exchange takes place. Sometimes written *stoma.*

Stramineous. Straw-colored.

Striate. Marked with fine longitudinal lines, grooves, furrows, or streaks.

Strict. Very straight and upright. (Figure 11-183.)

STRICT *(Fig. 11-183)*

Strigillose. Like *strigose* but hairs very short.

Strigose. With appressed stiff, rather short hairs. (Figure 11-184.)

STRIGOSE *(Fig. 11-184)*

Strophiole. An appendage at the *hilum* of some seeds.

Style. The usually stalk-like part of a pistil connecting the ovary and stigma. See *ovary* for drawing.

Sub. A prefix meaning either "almost" or "below."

Subtending. Situated closely beneath something, often enclosing or embracing it.

Subulate. Awl-shaped; narrowly triangular and tapering to a sharp
point. (Figure 11-185.)

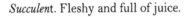

SUBULATE *(Fig. 11-185)*

subulate
leaf

Succulent. Fleshy and full of juice.

Sucker. A vegetative shoot arising from near or below the
ground.

Suffruticose. Low-shrubby; applied to perennials, the lower
part of the stems woody but the upper part *herbaceous.*
Also written *suffrutescent.*

Sulcate. Grooved or furrowed, especially if the groove is deep and
longitudinal. (Figure 11-186.)

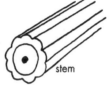

SULCATE *(Fig. 11-186)*

stem

Sulcus (pl. *sulci*). A furrow or groove. See *sulcate.*

Surculose-proliferous. Producing runners or offsets from the
base or from *rootstocks.*

Suture. A junction or seam of union; a
line of dehiscence. (Figure 11-187.)

SUTURE *(Fig. 11-187)*

suture

Taproot. The primary root continuing the axis of the plant
downward. Such roots may be thick or comparatively
thin. (Figure 11-188.)

TAPROOT *(Fig. 11-188)*

Tawny. Dull yellowish with a tinge of
brown.

Taxon (pl. *taxa*). A general term for
any morphological unit or group.

taproot

Teeth. Pointed protuberances or divisions of a structure.

Terete. Circular in cross-section and more or less elongated. Like cylindrical but may be slightly tapering. (Figure 11-189.)

TERETE *(Fig. 11-189)*

Ternate. Arranged in three's.

Terrestrial. A plant growing in the air with its basal parts in the soil. Compare *aquatic.*

Tesselate. The surface marked with square or oblong depressions.

Tetra-angular. With four angles.

Thyrse. A contracted, cylindrical, or ovoid-pyramidal usually densely flowered *panicle*, like a cluster of grapes. Also written *thrysus.*

Tiller. A lateral shoot, basal or subterranean, more or less erect. Compare *rhizome* and *stolon.* (Figure 11-190.)

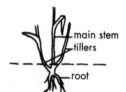

TILLER *(Fig. 11-190)*

Tomentose. With a dense, wool-like covering of matted, intertangled hairs of medium length. Compare *lanate* and *canescent.* (Figure 11-191.)

TOMENTOSE *(Fig. 11-191)*

Tomentulose. Sparingly or minutely *tomentose.*

Tomentum. The covering of closely interwoven and tangled hairs in a tomentose surface.

Trailing. Prostrate but not rooting.

Translucent. Transmitting rays of light without being actually transparent.

Tree. A perennial woody plant of considerable stature at maturity and with one or few main trunks. Rather loosely used but, strangely enough, a fairly well-understood concept. (Figure 11-192.)

TREE *(Fig. 11-192)*

Triad. A group of three adjacent structures as the three spikelets at a rachis node in Hordeum. (Figure 11-193.)

TRIAD *(Fig. 11-193)*

Trichome. A hairlike outgrowth of the epidermis.

Trifid. Divided into three parts as in the awn of *Aristida.* (Figure 11-194.)

TRIFID *(Fig. 11-194)*

Trigonal. Three-angled. (Figure 11-195.)

TRIGONAL *(Fig. 11-195)*

Trigonous. Three-angled. Same as *trigonal.*

Triquetrous. With three salient angles, the sides concave or channeled. (Figure 11-196.)

TRIQUETROUS *(Fig. 11-196)*

149

Truncate. Squared at the tip or base as if cut off with a straight blade. (Figure 11-197.)

TRUNCATE *(Fig. 11-197)*

apex   base

Tube. Any hollow cylindrical structure.

Tubercle. A small rounded structure, often pimple-like. (Figure 11-198.)

Tuberculate. Bearing small processes or *tubercles.*

TUBERCLES *(Fig. 11-198)*

Tufted. Having a cluster of hairs or other slender outgrowths; stems in a very close cluster.

Tumid. Swollen.

Tunicated. Having concentric coats, as an onion bulb. See *bulb* for drawing.

Turbinate. Top-shaped; inversely conical. About the same as obconical. See *obconical* for drawing.

Turgid. Swollen or tightly drawn, said of a thin covering expanded by internal pressure.

Turion. A scaly, often succulent shoot produced from a bud on an underground *rootstock.*

Type. In taxonomy, the specimen or specimens from which the original description was made.

Umbel. A convex or flat-topped inflorescence, the flowers all arising from one point. (Figure 11-199.)

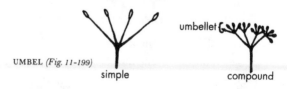

umbellet

UMBEL *(Fig. 11-199)*

simple   compound

Umbellate. In or like an *umbel.*

Umbellet. A small or secondary *umbel* in a compound umbel. See *umbel* for drawing.

Umbonate. Bearing a stout projection in the center; bossed. (Figure 11-200.)

UMBONATE *(Fig. 11-200)*

Uncinate. Hooked near the apex or in the form of a hook. (Figure 11-201.)

UNCINATE *(Fig. 11-201)*

uncinate bristle

Undershrub. A small low shrub or a perennial plant woody only at the base.

Undulate. The margin gently wavy. Same as *repand.* Compare *sinuate.* (Figure 11-202.)

Unilateral. Arranged on one side.

Uniseriate. Arranged in one row or series.

Unisexual. With either stamens or pistils, but not both. Compare *bisexual* and *perfect.*

UNDULATE *(Fig. 11-202)*

Utricle. A small, thin-walled, rather bladder-like, one-seeded fruit.

Vaginate. Provided with or surrounded by a *sheath.*

Valve. One of the parts or segments into which a *dehiscent* fruit splits.

Vascular bundle. An elongated group of cells specialized for conduction and often support. In a leaf or bract, the veins, nerves or ribs.

Vein. Threads of vascular tissue in a leaf or other organ, especially those which branch. Compare *nerve.*

Ventral. Belonging to the inner or axis side of an organ; hence the upper surface of a leaf.

Ventricose. Inflated or swollen unequally, as on one side. (Figure 11-203.)

VENTRICOSE *(Fig. 11-203)*

Vernation. The particular arrangement of a leaf or its parts in the bud.

Verrucose. Covered with wart-like elevations. (Figure 11-204.)

VERRUCOSE *(Fig. 11-204)*

Versatile. An anther attached at or near its middle and turning freely on its support. Compare *basifixed*. (Figure 11-205.)

VERSATILE *(Fig. 11-205)*

Verticillate. With three or more leaves or other structures arranged in a circle about a stem or other common axis. Same as *whorled*.

Verticils. A circle of three or more structures around a common axis.

Vestigial. Rudimentary or very reduced.

Villous. With long, soft, somewhat wavy hairs. Compare *pilose*. (Figure 11-206.)

VILLOUS *(Fig. 11-206)*

Vine. A plant climbing or scrambling on some support, the stem not standing upright of itself.

Virgate. Wandlike, as a slender, straight, erect stem.

Viscid. Glutinous, sticky, or gummy to the touch.

Viviperous. A type of reproduction involving modified bracts of the reproductive organs, but not from seeds. A special type of vegetative reproduction. (Figure 11-207.)

VIVIPEROUS *(Fig. 11-207)*

normal   viviperous

Wanting. Lacking, used especially of a structure often present.

Web. The cluster of fine, soft, crinkly, or folded hairs at the base of the lemmas as in some species of *Poa.* (Figure 11-208.)

WEB *(Fig. 11-208)*

Weed. A troublesome or aggressive plant that intrudes where not wanted, especially a plant that vigorously colonizes disturbed areas. To the rangeman, however, a weed is any herbaceous, non-grasslike plant on the range.

Whorled. With three or more leaves or other structures arranged in a circle around a stem or some common axis. Same as *verticillate.*

Wing. Any membranous or thin expansion bordering or surrounding an organ. (Figure 11-209.)

WING *(Fig. 11-209)*

Winged. Provided with wings.

Wing-margined. With a *very* narrow wing. (Figure 11-210.)

WING-MARGINED *(Fig. 11-210)*

Winter annual. A plant where the seed germinates in the fall, the seedling surviving the winter and completing its growth in the spring of the next season.

Woolly. With long, soft, interwoven hair. Same as *lanate.* See *lanate* for drawing.

Xeric. See *xerophytic.*

Xerophyte. A plant adapted to *xerophytic* conditions.

Xerophytic. Adapted to dry or arid habitats. Compare *mesophyte* and *hydrophyte.*

CPSIA information can be obtained
at www.ICGtesting.com
Printed in the USA
LVHW100811230123
737559LV00002B/30